Two Shall Become One

*Preparation for Engaged Couples,
and Refreshment for Marriage*

By John and Rynner Mann

Two Shall Become One
© 2002 By John and Rynner Mann
Calvary Chapel Publishing

ISBN 0-9700218-4-4

Printed in the United States of America.

Photography: Jim Sisco

To our parents.
Thank you for showing us
the meaning of commitment.

To Pastor Chuck Smith.
Without your solid Biblical teaching,
this book never could have been written.
May the Lord bless you
for your faithfulness.

Foreword

We have had the privilege of ministering to married couples for over fifteen years at Calvary Chapel in Costa Mesa, California. We lead a weekly fellowship for married couples as well as a six-week class for engaged couples entitled, "Two Shall Become One." The inspiration for this book has come from teaching these classes. Through the years we have seen many couples struggle in marriage due in part to a lack of preparation and commitment. We wanted to provide engaged couples with a book based on Biblical principles, and a tool for married couples to refresh their love for one another.

This book has its origin in the cassette tapes taken from the premarital class John taught. Hence, we have used the pronoun "I" in place of "we" in some cases in the context of the book. Also, to avoid additional tedium regarding the usage of the word fiancé (male) and fiancée (female), we have chosen to use the word fiancée when both are addressed at the same time.

Contents

Introduction

God created the institution of marriage, and we are so glad that you have taken a step to see what He has to say about it! It is a wonderful adventure, but it is also a great responsibility. In the months to come, you will be making hundreds of decisions regarding your wedding and reception, but remember: *After every wedding comes a marriage*. This is the most important decision you will make in your life next to receiving Jesus Christ as your Savior. You want to make sure of your decision to marry this person because it is a commitment life.

The Lord wants and needs to be the center of your relationship. The Bible says, "Two are better than one…and a threefold cord is not quickly broken" (Ecclesiastes 4:9,12). Since God ordained marriage, He wants to help you on the road to becoming one flesh. He desires to guide you, and give you the joy that overflows from a Christ-centered relationship. The Word instructs you to "Trust in the LORD with all your heart, and lean not on your own understanding; in all your ways acknowledge Him, and He shall direct your paths" (Proverbs 3:5,6). He will give you the direction you need for your future decisions as you go to Him in prayer in everything: from where to go on your honeymoon to where to live, and how many children to have!

If you are married, we pray that this book will refresh your relationship in areas where you may have struggled. We hope it will rekindle that love that brought the two of you together. The Lord will certainly bless your efforts and desire to keep your marriage alive.

After you have answered the questions at the end of each chapter, spend time discussing them together. Take your fiancée or spouse out for coffee, or meet after church to share your answers. If you are honest with each other regarding your past, present, and desires for your future, God will bless your relationship and give you a solid foundation upon which to build your marriage.

We pray that the Lord will richly bless you and your commitment to one another!

John and Rynner Mann

CHAPTER 1

In The Beginning

The First Wedding

In the beginning God created man, and He saw that he was not complete. God knew that Adam would not make a good bachelor so He created Eve to bring love, beauty, and companionship to him. God ordained marriage by presiding over the first wedding in the Garden of Eden. It was the first garden wedding, and what a beautiful sight it must have been to behold! Just imagine the variety of flowers, the verdant landscape, and the assorted fruit platters they might have had at the reception. God brought Eve to Adam and she became his wife. The Bible says:

> It is not good that man should be alone; I will make him a helper comparable to him. Out of the ground the LORD God formed every beast of the field and every bird of the air, and brought them to Adam to see what he would call them. And whatever Adam called each living creature, that was its name. So Adam gave names to all cattle, to the birds of the air, and to every beast of the field. But for Adam there was not found a helper comparable to him. And the LORD God caused a deep sleep to fall on Adam, and he slept; and He took one of his ribs, and closed up the flesh in its place. Then the rib which the LORD God had taken from man He made into a woman, and He brought her to the man. And Adam said: "This is now bone of my bones and flesh of my flesh; she shall be called Woman, because she was taken out of Man." Therefore a man shall leave his father and mother and be joined to his wife, and they shall become one flesh. And they were both naked, the man and his wife, and were not ashamed. (Genesis 2:18-25)

How blessed Adam was to have a wife that would complete him. God also knows just the right type of person to complete you! You may have certain criteria as to what you are looking for in a spouse, but God knows what you need. He will give you someone that complements you. He has our best interests in mind, and He will do "exceedingly abundantly above all that we [could] ask or think, according to the power that works in us" (Ephesians 3:20).

A Gift From God

When Eve was created for her husband, we find that God did not take a part of the head of Adam so that he would dominate over her, nor did He take a part of his foot to be stepped on by him. God took a rib from his side, from underneath his arm. It was taken from the place nearest to his heart, so that he could protect Eve, and become a covering for her. God was entrusting a very special gift to Adam.

The Bible says, "Every good gift and every perfect gift is from above, and comes down from the Father of lights, with whom there is no variation or shadow of turning" (James 1:17). Think of your fiancée as a gift from the Lord. God has entrusted you with this gift, and you are to take care of it! Think of a tangible item that means a lot to you. Let's say men, that you were given a car as a present for graduation. What did you do with it when you first received it? You took care of it, you polished it, and you waxed it. You probably had the interior detailed regularly, and made sure that the engine always had enough oil. You gave attention to every working detail. You were proud of that new car. Even though a woman is much more precious than any item you could possess, the concept is the same. She is a gift! God has given her to you to love, and to serve, and you should want to take care of her.

I remember how the Lord brought that special gift to me over twenty years ago. Rynner and I first met at The Good Earth Restaurant, following the College and Career Fellowship at our church. I was very attracted to her. Subsequently, we found ourselves at a home fellowship that was an offshoot of the bigger group. I prayed that first night, "Lord, if we can get to know each other, or if she is the one for me, could you have her get up from the sofa after the study and talk to me?" I wanted to make sure the relationship was of the Lord. What is amazing is, after the study she got up from the sofa, and came over to ask me for prayer! The Lord brought her to me even as the Scripture said God brought Eve to Adam. Take comfort in this: if God has brought your fiancée to you, you can be sure that He has wonderful plans and blessings for your future! He knows what you need to complete your life. Let's face it, guys, we are boring by ourselves. We need a woman to bring us joy and excitement; they add spice to life.

Adam said, "This is now bone of my bones and flesh of my flesh; she shall be called Woman, because she was taken out of Man" (Genesis 2:23). The Bible also says, "A man shall leave his father and mother and be joined to his wife, and the two shall become one flesh" (Ephesians 5:31). God brought Adam and Eve together to be one flesh. From the first day you put that engagement ring on the finger of your fiancée, God has been molding and shaping your lives to become one flesh. This is a continual process; it does not happen overnight. It takes time to take two people with diverse lifestyles and backgrounds, and make them *one*. We need to have patience with one another as God is doing His work by His Spirit.

Leave and Cleave

There are a couple of aspects to keep in mind, as we become one flesh. First, we need to leave and cleave. God addressed the man first, however we both need to leave our parents as well as former relationships, and we need to cleave to our spouse. Maybe we are attached to our parents for the advice they give us, or maybe our mom would love to be an integral part of our life even after we are married. Perhaps we have been close to a former roommate or colleague. Once we are married we need to set these secondary relationships aside. We need to establish our own household because these relationships can cause potential conflicts or problems in the future. The following *Dear Abby* letter applies to this directly:

> **Dear Abby:** I am writing with a message of warning to newlywed wives. When I first married "Jim," I used to spend hours after dinner every night on the phone with my mother

talking about family news-what was happening with my father, my sister, my sister's husband, etc. When Jim complained, my mother and I both felt he was being selfish and ignored him.

Soon Jim took up jogging, and as soon as I picked up the phone in the evening, he would leave the house to run his miles. Then Jim started traveling to races on the weekends and eventually met "Peggy," a pretty school teacher from a neighboring town who also liked to jog. My inability to "let go" and build my primary family ties with my new husband cost me a great guy. How do I know he's so great? Because he still waves to my mother and me when we see him in the park jogging with Peggy and their two beautiful daughters.

Out of the Race in N.J.

Dear Out: I'm printing your cautionary tale for all to see. How sad that your preoccupation with your family caused you to shut out the person with whom you vowed to build a life. I find it interesting that when your ex-husband sees you in the park, you're still with your mother. Unless that is the way you want it to be for the rest of your life, I recommend some counseling.[1]

What a warning for all of us! It is unfortunate that this woman put her relationship with her mother before her husband. He felt left out, and so he looked elsewhere for fulfillment. We know Biblically that his actions cannot be justified, but it does illustrate the importance of leaving the relationship of our family members as we know it now, and cleaving to our spouse.

The Bible says, "Therefore shall a man leave his father and his mother, and shall cleave unto his wife: and they shall be one flesh" (Genesis 2:24 KJV). What does it mean to cleave? The Hebrew word implies "to glue together, or to join oneself to another closely." That is what happens when we become one flesh. If we know anyone who has been through a divorce, we know how wrenching that can be. Think of marriage as two sheets of plywood that are glued together to provide strength. If the top layer of wood were to be pulled off in order to separate the pieces, it would not come off all at once. There would be some pieces still stuck together. That is what happens with divorce. Something from each person is left with the other, especially if there are children involved.

Marriage is a *oneness* that occurs when each spouse is fully committed to the other. The feeling of this bond may not occur overnight, because becoming one is a process. But it is a blessing too! There is no more driving home separately after church and no longer a need for late night phone calls. We get to share everything with our spouse.

Confession Session

In the secular community, one out of every two marriages ends in divorce. In recent days, studies have indicated that among evangelical Christians one out of every two marriages ends in divorce as well. What a sad indictment! An encouraging statistic reveals that when couples pray together on a regular basis, the ratio changes from *one out of two* to one out of every *one thousand and fifty-two* marriages ending in divorce.[2] When we pray together as couples, we have to ask for cleansing from our sin. The Lord says, "If I regard iniquity in my heart, the Lord will not hear [me]" (Psalm 66:18). The Bible also says, "Confess your trespasses to one another, and pray for one another, that you may be healed. The effective, fervent prayer of a righteous man avails much" (James 5:16). We can see from these verses that if we want to have a time of prayer with our fiancée or spouse, it is important that we have a clean slate with God. We cannot let sin or bitterness reside in our hearts. We have to confess it to each other before we pray, or the Lord will not hear us. Prayer in a marriage can be so powerful! Men, another Scripture to keep in mind is:

> Likewise you husbands, dwell with [your wives] with understanding, giving honor to the wife, as to the weaker vessel, and as being heirs together of the grace of life, that *your prayers may not be hindered.* (1 Peter 3:7)[Emphasis mine.]

Sin can hinder the efficacy of our prayers. We need to be confessing our faults and sins, and praying together daily.

Genesis says, "And they were both naked, the man and his wife, and were not ashamed" (Genesis 2:25). Adam and Eve were unclothed before the Lord and they did not think anything about it. How idyllic it was for them not to have to deal with the sin factor. In the third chapter of Genesis, we find that they sinned by eating of the fruit; they became ashamed, and they tried to hide from God. Sin had separated them from the Lord. We also need to be aware of the fact that sin will separate us from each other. What we do will affect our relationship with the Lord and one another. We are "not our own," or a separate entity after we become one with our spouse. (See 1 Corinthians 6:19.)

It is also important for us to be able to be emotionally and spiritually open with one another. When Rynner and I got engaged, the Lord allowed us to have what we call "a confession session." We shared our lives up until the time we met, where we had stumbled, and the weak areas with which God was still working. The Lord really used this in our lives! Now, when a problem arises in our relationship, we are there to pray for each other, to hold one another up, and to encourage each other in our weaknesses. There are no surprises. We do not have to hide, or try to face the challenges of life alone. That is not marriage! When we are open with one another, the enemy does not have a foothold. He cannot cause us to continue in our sin; thereby keeping us bound in it! (See James 5:16.)

We may think, "Of course, when we are married, we will share with one another." It is surprising to see the number of couples I have counseled who hide areas of their lives from their spouses! A few months ago, I received a call from a young married woman who had just ended an affair with another man. She asked me if I thought she should tell her husband. I told her she needed to tell him, and I also shared the importance of confessing and forgiving one another. She then proceeded to tell me that she had had another affair earlier in their marriage with a different man, and she never confessed it to her husband. Now, she was afraid that she would have to tell him about both relationships, and she wondered if he would forgive her. Do you see how important honesty is in a marriage from the beginning, and throughout the relationship? If she had told her spouse about the initial affair (not to mention the feelings and circumstances that led up to it), perhaps the subsequent affair would have been avoided.

Now, you may be saying, "My fiancée does not really know what I have gone through; they do not really know who I am, and I am not sure I want to tell them." If you can say this, you are on shaky ground today in your relationship. If the person you are going to marry does not know who you really are, is that fair to them? Are you wearing a mask? We are never to wear a mask with the one with whom we have pledged to live the rest of our lives! One of the greatest joys in marriage is that when our fiancée or spouse asks us how we are doing, we do not have to say, "I am doing just fine." We can say, "I am not doing well at all; please pray for me!" We can share *whatever* is going on; we can be open and honest. That is how the Lord created marriage! We have someone with whom we can bear our burden, and someone with whom we can pray. If we keep secrets from one another, we are only giving the enemy a stronghold in our lives, to continue in incorrect or sinful behavior.

Share Who You Are

A man may say, "If I tell my fiancée who I really am, or what I struggle with, she may break off the engagement." Let me tell you here and now: she will probably find out who you are, and what you have done one way or another. The Bible says, "be sure your sin will find you out" (Numbers 32:23). Wouldn't it be better to pray about it now with the Lord, to come before her on a platform of humility, and ask forgiveness? I will tell you that it is much easier for the fiancée to go home to pray about it *before* she has a wedding ring on her finger, than it is for her to feel deceived after the wedding vows have been exchanged. By not telling her your problems and struggles now, you are just opening yourself and your spouse to pain later on. It is guaranteed! There should be no secrets between a husband and a wife.

We recently counseled a woman who was planning to get married in the near future. She asked us whether or not she should reveal that she was molested when she was a little girl. We asked her what her reasons were for keeping it from her fiancé. She said she did not want to burden him with the information. Rynner said, "What if you should see this person after you are married with your husband present?

Would you feel uncomfortable?" She said, "Yes." We prayed for her, and asked the Lord to show her what He wanted her to do. The woman came back to us the next week, and told us that she could not get the thought out of her mind, and that she felt the Lord was prompting her to share her story with her fiancé. After she told him, she said she felt so relieved, and as if a tremendous burden had been lifted off of her shoulders. We asked her fiancé what he thought about what she shared. He said, "I was encouraged that I could bear her burden with her, and I could not imagine her going through life without sharing with me what had happened." He also said that he felt closer to her because of it.

Now, it should be noted that we have read several engagement books, and one book we read advocated not telling your fiancée about your past. The author stated that it would be inflicting pain on the other person. Well, wouldn't you want to receive all of the information you could about your fiancée now rather than later? If they did find out about a former marriage, an abortion, imprisonment, or even smaller shortcomings like a chronic love for shopping, or a problem with overeating, do you think your fiancée would be hurt if you did not tell them now? This could open a whole host of problems two or three years into your marriage. The first thing the violated spouse would say is, "What else have you been keeping from me? Who are you really? And couldn't you have trusted me enough to tell me before we were married?" We have to think seriously about the ramifications of the choices we make. Dealing with these issues now is so much wiser and less stressful for both of you, than waiting until a later time. Your fiancée can take it to the Lord in prayer, forgive you, and pray for you! At the outset, a broken engagement is much better to have now, than having a painful breakup and a divorce later.

It is important that we share our history and weak areas with our fiancée or spouse. However, we are not advocating that we dwell on the past, or go into specific detail concerning our sin unless the Lord directs us. The Apostle Paul said:

> But one thing I do, forgetting those things which are behind
> and reaching forward to those things which are ahead, I press
> toward the goal for the prize of the upward call of God in
> Christ Jesus. (Philippians 3:13,14)

The past might be painful, but we need to share who we are with one another and then leave it behind. We should not continue to bring it up. We are not to keep a record of wrongs. If you get into a pattern of not sharing now, you will take that behavior into your marriage, and it could be detrimental to your relationship. It will become easier and easier to hide, make you more vulnerable, and increase the likelihood of falling into sin.

Let me give you an example. Let's say you have a problem with pornography, and you do not share that with your fiancée before you get married. You say to yourself, "I know this is wrong, and I should confess it because it is bringing division into our relationship. But she does not know, and I will not tell her." If you continue this way, your problem will only become worse. If, in the beginning you say, "This is what I have gone through and how I am struggling. You can take me or leave me. I want victory over this area of my life as I surrender these areas daily to the Lord. If you will come alongside me and encourage me, I know I can get through it. If you have any weak areas, I will be there for you as well. We can pray for each other for victory." I am not saying that you absolutely must have a confession session. I am only pointing out that many of those who have chosen to have a time of confessing the weaknesses and sins of the past with each other have grown deeper in their love and commitment to one another. A young woman in our premarital class came to me after she and her fiancé had a time of sharing with each other, and she said it was "so freeing" to open up, and not to have anything hidden between them. She said that she felt "born again" all over because she had finally opened up to someone, and he accepted her for who she really was.

Rynner and I can say, after almost twenty years of marriage, that we do not have any secrets between us. We have nothing to fear; no subject will come up between us where we feel nervous or ashamed. I know everything about her past and present, and she knows everything about mine. It is a beautiful thing to be able to be ourselves with the person God has given to us for life. We accept each other for who we are. It is a great feeling of intimate freedom!

Review Questions

In the Beginning

1. What is your definition of marriage?

   Joining of two people to come as one to spend the rest of
   their lives together in the spirit of the lord

2. List the reasons you are marrying your fiancée, or the reasons you married your spouse.

   We can be ourselves with each other. We feel comfortable
   with each other

3. What kind of helper did God design the woman to be?

   A supporter, Encourger,

4. What does it mean for a wife to complement her husband?

Being what her husband needs to uplift him
She makes him better than what he really is !!

5. **Women**: List specific ways in which you can complement or help your fiancé or spouse. **Men**: List specific ways in which you would like to be complemented or helped by your fiancée or spouse.

6. What does it mean to "leave [your] father and [your] mother" (Ephesians 5:31)?

To lean upon your Spouse to make your spouse
your family.

7. The Bible says, "Therefore a man shall leave his father and mother and be joined to his wife, and they shall become one flesh" (Genesis 2:24). List some of the ways that you can preserve this *oneness* in your marriage.

a) _Prayer, reading of the bible_
Confession
Trust
Communication

b) _____

_____

_____

_____

c) _____

_____

_____

_____

d) _____

_____

_____

_____

e) _____

_____

_____

_____

8. What does it mean to cleave?

to glue together or to join oneself to another closely

9. Read Matthew 19:4-6. Share your thoughts regarding verse 6, and your commitment to marriage.

_____

_____

_____

_____

10. Confessing our sins to each other is an important part of maintaining a healthy marriage. Why is this important?

_____

_____

_____

_____

_____

11. Is there any information you have kept from your fiancée or spouse that could become a hindrance to your relationship?

_____

_____

_____

_____

_____

12. List three Bible verses you would like to memorize in order to strengthen your relationship.

a) _____

_____

_____

_____

b) _____

_____

_____

_____

c) _____

_____

_____

Notes

_____

_____

_____

_____

_____

_____

_____

_____

_____

_____

_____

_____

_____

_____

_____

_____

_____

_____

_____

_____

_____

_____

_____

Notes

_____

_____

_____

_____

_____

_____

_____

_____

_____

_____

_____

_____

_____

_____

_____

_____

_____

_____

_____

_____

_____

_____

CHAPTER 2

The Roles of the Husband and Wife

Submit to One Another

One of the most quoted Scriptures on marriage is found in Ephesians Chapter Five. It teaches about the importance of submission in our relationships. It says:

> Submitting to one another in the fear of God. Wives, submit to your own husbands, as to the Lord. For the husband is head of the wife, as also Christ is head of the church; and He is the Savior of the body. Therefore, just as the church is subject to Christ, so let the wives be to their own husbands in everything. Husbands, love your wives, just as Christ also loved the church and gave Himself for it, that He might sanctify and cleanse it with the washing of water by the word, that He might present it to Himself a glorious church, not having spot or wrinkle or any such thing, but that it should be holy and without blemish. So husbands ought to love their own wives as their own bodies; he who loves his wife loves himself. For no one ever hated his own flesh, but nourishes and cherishes it, just as the Lord does the church. For we are members of His body, of His flesh and of His bones. "For this reason a man shall leave his father and mother and be joined to his wife, and the two shall become one flesh." This is a great mystery, but I speak concerning Christ and the church. Nevertheless let each one of you in particular so love his own wife as himself, and let the wife see that she respects her husband. (Ephesians 5:21-33)

We are to submit ourselves to one another in the fear of God. What does it mean to submit? There are two words in the New Testament that describe the role of submission between a husband and a wife. The word *hupotasso* is a military term that means "to arrange in military fashion under the command of a leader." In a nonmilitary sense, it speaks of "a voluntary attitude of giving or cooperating, assuming responsibility, or carrying a burden." The other word for submission is *hupeiko*. This means "to resist no longer, to give way, or to yield to authority." In submitting to one another, we yield. Men, this does not mean that your fiancée is the only one who submits! I have talked to many men who have said, "My wife is to submit to me! That is what the Bible teaches." They are obviously referring to the verse that says, "Wives, submit to your own husbands, as to the Lord" (Ephesians 5:22). They neglect to notice verse 21 that says we are to submit "to one another in the fear of God." The husband makes the final decision because he has the ultimate authority. When making decisions, he needs to listen to his wife, value her input, and her opinions.

There is a chain of command taught in the Bible: God is the head of the home; the husband falls under the authority of the Lord, and the wife under the husband. The children, in turn, are under the authority of the parents. If you are an engaged man and you think, "The home is going to be MY domain, I am going to rule in it, and my wife is going to obey ME!" You are wrong, wrong, wrong! We submit one to another. You are not to force your wife to submit, but we are to submit to one another in love. As you love her "as Christ loved the church, and gave himself for it," she will want to submit to you! Some of the greatest ideas for your future will come from your wife. Listen to what she has to say, and you will be blessed. I know of men who have failed to benefit from the wisdom and insight of their wives. One example is a man I know who wanted to buy a van from a private party. His wife said that she did not have a good feeling about it, and asked him not to buy it. He assured her that to purchase the vehicle was the right course of action, and he proceeded to put down the deposit. He subsequently went to the bank to get the balance of the money he needed. When he went back to the home of the party selling the van, he could not find them there, nor could he find proof that they had ever lived in that home. It was a scam! We as men need to listen to our wives, because God can use them to keep us out of trouble.

Husbands Are Called to Lead

The woman was not created to be the leader. In our relationships, and ultimately our marriage, one will rise to be the leader; it usually is the one with the strongest personality. I want to encourage you men to do your own study in the Word of God regarding your role as a husband. If you abdicate your role as the leader, your wife will become the head of the home. There are many wives I have talked to who do not want to be the leader, but feel that it has been thrust upon them out of necessity. This can create resentment and bitterness on the part of the wife. The Lord has given us as men the role of the leader, and we need to fulfill our responsibility.

Wives Submit to Your Husbands

Many of the problems in marriages are a result of couples vying for the leadership role. The Bible gives clear instruction to the wives, and that is to "submit to your own husbands, as to the Lord," and also to "respect [your] husband" (Ephesians 5:22,33). You can voice your opinion in a loving way, but you need to respect and support the final decision made by your husband.

Jesus Christ made Himself subject to the will of the Father. He said, "Abba, Father, all things are possible for You. Take this cup away from Me; nevertheless, not what I will, but what You will" (Mark 14:36). We are to submit to one another in the same way. We yield, or we give way to the desire of our fiancée or spouse. I have had men come into my office and say, "She is not submitting to me, or obeying me. It is my job to chasten her." They feel it is their duty to mold and shape their wives. We are not called to try to perform the job of the Holy Spirit in the lives of one another. God is the one who changes us. The greatest way to change a person is not to say a word. We need to encourage our fiancée or our spouse in the areas where they have strengths, and then pray for their weak areas. (See Philippians 4:6-8.) God can change them! How many of us respond to discouragement? When someone says what we do not want to hear, it makes us run the other way, doesn't it? Conversely, when we are encouraged, we can accomplish great things. Do you remember being involved in sports in high school or college? The stands were filled with people cheering, not to mention the cheerleaders, and your parents. You responded to their encouragement, and it made you want to do better. We also need to encourage each other in marriage. We know that in the area of submission, the husband makes the final decision. Let's say that, as a woman, you have articulated your feelings to your husband regarding what you think is right, and he says, "Thank you so much for sharing those thoughts, but I think we will go with my initial plan." At this point, if you still feel your way is the best course of action, you need to pray. You need to support your husband because ultimately he is responsible before the Lord. Do not worry, God will take care of you! The goal for the wife is not to be right, or even to save the situation; the goal of the wife is to submit, as unto the Lord.

The Bible says, "For the husband is head of the wife, as also Christ is head of the church; and He is the Savior of the body" (Ephesians 5:23). Women, you are to submit to your own husband, but this does not require you to submit to anything that would compromise your walk with the Lord, or violate your conscience in any way. The Scriptures declare, "Wives, submit to your own husbands, as is fitting in the Lord" (Colossians 3:18). It also says:

> Likewise you wives, be submissive to your own husbands, that even if some do not obey the word, they, without a word, may be won by the conduct of their wives, when they observe your chaste conduct accompanied by fear. Do not let your beauty be that outward adorning of arranging the hair, of wearing gold, or of putting on fine apparel; but let it be the hidden person of the heart, with the incorruptible ornament of a gentle and quiet spirit, which is very precious in the sight of God. For in this manner, in former times, the holy women who trusted in God also adorned themselves, being submissive to their own husbands, as Sarah obeyed Abraham, calling him lord, whose daughters you are if you do good and are not afraid with any terror. (1 Peter 3:1-6)

What this Scripture is saying is that if the husband is a nonbeliever, he can be won to Christ by the behavior of the wife. We have a friend who received Christ as her Savior after she was married. Her husband is still a nonbeliever, but she is compliant to his desires. He loves her, and they get along great as long as she does not talk about the Lord. He allows her to go to church if she will plan to be home when he arises on Sunday morning. She attends the first service, and then she cooks a nice breakfast for him. He does not prefer her to be out in the evenings or on the weekends unless he is out of town, and she is obedient to him. After thirty-two years of marriage, he recently suggested that they attend one of the services at our church. She was so excited! Although he is not a believer yet, her behavior is certainly blessing and affecting him. She is submitting to her husband, as unto the Lord.

Do Not Be Unequally Yoked

The Scripture says that a spouse can be won to the Lord without a word, but this does not give us license to marry a nonbeliever willfully. Paul said:

> Do not be unequally yoked together with unbelievers. For what fellowship has righteousness with lawlessness? And what communion has light with darkness? And what accord has Christ with Belial? Or what part has a believer with an unbeliever? And what agreement has the temple of God with idols? For you are the temple of the living God. As God has said: "I will dwell in them and walk among them. I will be their God, and they shall be My people." Therefore "Come out from among them and be separate, says the Lord. Do not touch what is unclean, and I will receive you. I will be a Father to you, and you shall be My sons and daughters, says the LORD Almighty." (2 Corinthians 6:14-18)

If you are engaged to a nonbeliever, you are heading down a very difficult path. I have met with many individuals who have been disobedient to the Word of God, and have married non-Christians. In the heat of the romance, they have neglected to think of what the future holds for them. When we marry a non-Christian, we do not have support in spiritual matters. Marriage can become a *nightmare*, and that is why the Lord instructs us against it. We may be saying, "I know they will come to Christ after we have been married." While this may be true, we do not want to disobey the Word of God, and take a chance! There is no instruction in the Bible for "missionary dating." What if they do not accept Christ? Where will we be in five or ten years? One woman I talked to several weeks ago was living in a situation just like this. After a Sunday service, she approached me for prayer with tears in her eyes, and said, "I want my husband to be the spiritual leader of our home, but he has only prayed with me once in twenty years!" This is not the ideal that God intends for marriage.

Even if we are both believers, we need to spiritually be of the same mind. I cannot tell you how many people I have talked to who have said, "I thought they were a Christian before I married them!" These are areas that need to be addressed *before* we get married. Amos 3:3 says, "Can two walk together, unless they are agreed?" We have to make sure our fiancée feels just as we feel about spiritual things. If you have a desire to go on the mission field, does your fiancée feel the same? Do they like to spend time in prayer like you do? Do they enjoy attending a Bible study during the week as well as a church service on Sunday? The Lord needs to take the first place in our lives, even before each other. Yes, the Lord has brought that special person into our life, but God needs to be above that relationship. He needs to be supreme in all of our hearts. "But seek first the kingdom of God and His righteousness, and all these things shall be added to you" (Matthew 6:33).

We Cannot Change One Another

We may think that our fiancée is not the way we would like them to be in some areas, but we think they will change. For example, a woman may say, "He is not the spiritual leader I desire him to be," or a man might say, "She is always challenging my every decision." We need to look at these areas of weakness, and say to ourselves, "If they never change in this area, would we still marry them?" The Lord, by His Holy Spirit, can and will change us. However, we should not go into marriage on the premise that our spouse will change right away. God does things according to His timing, and if we are not willing to do things His way, we might find ourselves very frustrated. (See Philippians 1:6 and Ecclesiastes 3:11a.) So often we try to play the part of the Holy Spirit in the lives of one another, and it just does not work. God wants to do the changing, because then He will get the glory!

We Are to be Servants

The Bible says, "Likewise you younger people, submit yourselves to your elders. Yes, all of you be submissive to one another, and be clothed with humility, for 'God resists the proud, but gives grace to the humble' " (1 Peter 5:5). It is so important that we grasp the importance of being a servant. The only way we can submit to one another in love is to be a servant and pray, "Lord, help me to do Your will, and not demand my own way. Show me how I can serve my spouse."

We also need to follow up this prayer with action. We cannot be all that God wants us to be on our own, because "[we] know that in [us] (that is, in [our] flesh) nothing good dwells" (Romans 7:18). We cannot be what God wants us to be without the power of His Holy Spirit working within us, and there are definite ways that we can foster this relationship with the Lord. We should be praying daily by ourselves, and with our fiancée or spouse. We should be reading the Word of God alone and together on a regular basis. We need to agree to consistently attend a church where the Bible is taught from Genesis to Revelation, and we need to be sharing our faith in Jesus Christ with others. These are Christian basics. All of these things will strengthen our walk with the Lord, they will aid us in becoming more like Christ, they will help us become servants to one another, and they will keep us from stumbling when temptation comes.

We know that engaged couples can be very busy with work, school, and with planning for their Big Day. But do not forget that *after every wedding comes a marriage*, and factoring God into our relationship is going to make a tremendous difference as the years pass. One couple I counseled was very busy, but the man told me that he would call his fiancée every day on her lunch hour at work, and they would spend time in prayer together on the phone. If they could not get together for a date or church in the evening, they would phone one another and read the Bible together responsively. (Reading responsively is when the man reads verse one, then the woman reads verse two, and so on through the chapter.) They made a conscious effort to put the Lord first in their relationship. When we choose to do these things they will, in turn, make it easier for us to continue the pattern in our marriages. The only way we can even begin to grasp the concept of being a servant in marriage is by allowing the Lord to work through us to bless the other person, and to put them before ourselves. This requires an active commitment on our part.

In the Old Testament, there were two kinds of servants: hired servants and bondservants. The hired servants were paid for their services, and they had certain rights, or liberties. Paul the apostle, on the other hand, referred to himself as the "servant of Jesus Christ" (Romans 1:1). The Greek word there is *doulos* which is bondservant or slave. The bondservant was a slave that did not receive wages, and he had no rights. By taking the title of a bondservant, Paul was saying, "Jesus is my master, and I am surrendered to Him, and His will for my life." This is the kind of attitude we need to take into our marriage relationship. This is especially true for men. We do not generally want to be a servant; we want to be the master, and the lord of our home.

Jesus was a servant. In the New Testament it says, "Let nothing be done through selfish ambition or conceit, but in lowliness of mind let each esteem others better than himself. Let each of you look out not only for his own interests, but also for the interests of others" (Philippians 2:3,4). Men, if you try to find ways to meet the needs of your wife, your home will run very smoothly. If you are looking to serve yourself, and are mainly concerned with how your wife can meet your needs, you are heading down a rough road. Women, you need to be servants, and prefer the needs of your husband before yourselves as well. The key phrase in this Scripture is "lowliness of mind," or, in other words, "being humble." Christ humbled Himself, and became a servant. We know of a great example of a husband who did just this: he humbled himself to minister to his wife. One night his wife had insomnia. After trying to fall back asleep for quite a while, she awakened her husband and told him she could not sleep. Instead of ignoring her, or telling her it was her problem and not to disturb him, do you know what he did? He cheerfully suggested that they go out to the kitchen, make ice cream malts, and watch *Anne of Green Gables* until she became drowsy. How do you think this made the wife feel? She loved it! She knew by the actions of her husband that he loved her, he wanted to minister to her, and put her needs before his own. In a very practical way, this man exemplified the verses in Philippians 2:3,4.

We are to lay down our lives for our wives. Jesus Christ is our example in this area. Paul goes on in Philippians to say:

> Let this mind be in you which was also in Christ Jesus, who, being in the form of God, did not consider it robbery to be equal with God, but made Himself of no reputation, taking the form of a servant, and coming in the likeness of men. And being found in appearance as a man, He humbled Himself and became obedient to the point of death, even the death of the cross. (Philippians 2:5-8)

Christ came down to earth, and took upon Himself the form of a servant. He was obedient unto death, and men, that is what we need to do as well. We need to take on the role of a servant. I think if more men would learn how to serve their wives in love, there would be fewer problems in marriages today!

Love Your Wife

The Bible says, "Husbands, love your wives, just as Christ also loved the church and gave Himself for it" (Ephesians 5:25). This is one of the most important verses for husbands. Men, let's face it, we can have a problem with pride. Selfishness can creep in, and we so often want our way. The Bible says:

> I have been crucified with Christ; it is no longer I who live, but Christ lives in me; and the life which I now live in the flesh I live by faith in the Son of God, who loved me and gave Himself for me. (Galatians 2:20)

We have to crucify our desires daily. What I mean by this is: men, you might come home from work, and have a desire to watch a football game, get on the computer, or do some yard work. But, you are married now. Your wife is at home when you get there, and she has needs as well. Remember it is not just you anymore. You need to eat meals with her, talk to her, and listen to her. Maybe she had a hard day, and she needs your undivided attention. The challenge is for you to focus on her needs for the evening, and not your own. If you had a hard day when you were single, you might have turned on the television, or played some basketball with the guys in order to relax. There is nothing wrong with recreation, but there needs to be a balance. You need to be aware of your responsibility as a husband, and seek to bless your spouse.

Let's look at another verse in Ephesians, "Nevertheless let each one of you in particular so love his own wife as himself, and let the wife see that she respects her husband" (Ephesians 5:33). The responsibility of the woman is to respect, or honor her husband. If we as men love our wives, and we will spiritually and physically lead them, they will respect us. We have to remember that the woman is a reflection of the man. They will respond to the way we treat them, and to the love and affection we have for them. Do you want your wife to love you? Then take the steps to love your wife. Conversely, do you want a nagging wife? Then ignore her, and that is what she will start to do! We are to love our wives as Christ loved the church, and gave Himself for it. This means that we are not to be a dictator, or to rule our homes with an iron fist. We are to care for our wives by guiding our homes with love and kindness.

Leading by Example

We need to also lead by example. Jesus said:

> You know that the rulers of the Gentiles lord it over them, and those who are great exercise authority over them. Yet it shall not be so among you; but whoever desires to become great among you, let him be your servant. And whoever desires to be first among you, let him be your slave- just as the Son of Man did not come to be served, but to serve, and to give His

life a ransom for many. (Matthew 20:25-28)

If we want to be the leaders God has called us to be, we need to reflect the character of Jesus, who taught us how to serve.

The Word of God says, "My little children, let us not love in word or in tongue, but in deed and in truth" (1 John 3:18). How true this Scripture is! I have talked with men who have supposedly walked with the Lord for ten years or so, and they still have a problem showing their wives that they love them by their actions. Oh, yes, they can say they love their wives, but are they showing that they love them by the way they treat them? These wives are grateful for gifts such as cards or flowers on occasion. But a wife will really know that her husband loves her when he listens to her with an attentive ear, when he is tender with her, and when he is sensitive to her needs. Peter talked about this sensitivity when he said:

> Likewise you husbands, dwell with [your wives] with understanding, giving honor to the wife, as to the weaker vessel, and as being heirs together of the grace of life, that your prayers may not be hindered. (1 Peter 3:7)

Men, you need to understand your wife, and what makes her tick. Study the way she communicates, and pick up on her idiosyncrasies. When you get to know her, you can dwell with her according to knowledge. You can even come to the point where you can tell her what she needs before she expresses it! That is really showing her that you love her.

After we are married, we may come home and say, "I have had a hard day. I am going to do my own thing this evening." I have seen so many marriages destroyed with this type of thinking. We need to know that this is not an option unless we both agree without reservation. One man told me that he came home one night from work with a few of his co-workers without the consent of his wife. They played cards and video games while she sat in the other room alone with the baby. This is not the ideal that God has for marriage! Another example is a woman who used to have "Girls' Night Out" once a week with her Christian friends. They ended up in a bar, and over the course of several weeks, this woman ended up having an affair with a man she had met that first evening. We need to make an effort to spend as much time as we can together. We are not "married singles." When we want to go out with our friends, we need to make sure we have the consent of our spouse, and their needs are being met. Believe me, we will reap the rewards! Before you get married, write a list of the things you like to do together. Do you like to play tennis, mountain bike, or walk on the beach? Find areas of common interest; they will serve to draw you closer as the years pass.

We as husbands need to initiate loving actions. The Scriptures say, "We love [God] because He first loved us" (1 John 4:19). We respond to the Lord because of all of the wonderful things He has done for us. He is the initiator. In the same way, we should not wait for our wives to make the first move toward being kind or helpful. If we have had an argument, we are not to get an attitude. Instead, we can use it as an opportunity to love them. We, as men, set the tone in our homes. We are not to wait for our wives to ask forgiveness; we need to make the first move. Even if they started the argument, our attitude was probably not flawless regarding the situation, so we can ask forgiveness for our shortcomings regarding what happened. If they had a hectic day at work, or with the children, we can find different ways to help them shoulder the load. Just because we are married now, it does not mean that our wives are going to do the grocery shopping, clean the house, give the dog a bath, do the laundry, pick up all of our shirts from the dry cleaners, and work full-time! If our wives choose to work, we need to be sensitive, and help them out in the home because we both live there. A friend of ours fills up both cars with gas on a weekly basis to help out his wife because she works. This is a way that we can show love! We can take out the trash without being asked three times. Our wives should not have to ask us to fix the lamp, or wash the car; we should just do it of our own volition. We are to minister to them like Jesus ministers to His church. We are to look for ways to help our wives, and to be a servant. The men are primarily addressed in this portion of Scripture, but that does not negate the responsibility of the wife to seek opportunities to be a servant to her husband as well.

Love Your Wife as You Love Yourself

Paul goes on to say, "So husbands ought to love their own wives as their own bodies; he who loves his wife loves himself. For no one ever hated his own flesh, but nourishes and cherishes it, just as the Lord does the church" (Ephesians 5:28,29). Men, do you take care of yourself? Do you take a shower regularly? Do you shave? Do you brush your teeth? Do you eat three meals a day? Do you work out at the gym in order to stay fit? Regarding your spiritual man: do you read the Bible daily? Do you go to church a couple of times a week to make sure you are getting spiritually fed? We need to apply all of these questions to our relationship with our wives. Remember Philippians 2:3,4 where we are to prefer their needs before our own? We are to make sure that our wives are taken care of first. We are to love our wives as we love ourselves.

God has given us a precious gift in our wives. We need to take care of them until the Lord returns, because we are accountable for these gifts. We are to be that spiritual leader, and the shepherd of our homes. We need to spend time reading the Bible with our wives. We need to worship the Lord together, and spend time in prayer. Men, we need to be the initiators. You can start doing this right now with your fiancée! You may think, "Oh, I do not have time now, but I plan to do it after we are married." Trust me, if you are not doing it now, you will not have time then. We have to make time whether we are married or not. We need to set patterns now; we need to be disciplined, and God will bless our efforts.

There is a Scripture about the virtuous woman in the Old Testament. It says, "Her husband is known in the gates, when he sits among the elders of the land" (Proverbs 31:23). Men, are you involved in a ministry at the church you attend? You need to remember that your first responsibility is your wife. She is the first ministry God has given you after your relationship with Him. If you have a great relationship with your wife, and your home is functioning smoothly, we would definitely recommend that you get involved at your church, teach Sunday School, or find a prayer meeting to attend. You will be blessed as you continue in the things of God. It is showing your wife that you have chosen to put Him first. By setting this example, she will reverence you and trust the decisions you make because she knows that you are in tune with the Lord, and she will find it easier to submit to you. Remember that you are the leader. The way the home is run is primarily up to you. If you will lead and love your wife the way the Lord has instructed you in Ephesians 5:21-33, you will have a peaceful and a joyful home. Your wife will honor and respect you, and you will have a marriage that will be a witness to others.

Review Questions

The Roles of the Husband and Wife

1. What is your definition of submission?

   _____

   _____

   _____

   _____

   _____

2. How do we submit to the Lord?

   _____

   _____

   _____

   _____

   _____

3. List some practical ways a wife can submit to her husband.

   _____

   _____

   _____

   _____

   _____

4. What is the Biblical role of the husband?

_____

_____

_____

_____

_____

5. What is the Biblical role of the wife?

_____

_____

_____

_____

_____

6. How can you help your future spouse fulfill his or her role?

_____

_____

_____

_____

_____

7. How can you practically apply Philippians 2:3,4 to your marriage?

_____

_____

_____

_____

_____

8. What does it mean to be unequally yoked? (See 2 Corinthians 6:14-18.)

_____

_____

_____

_____

_____

9. Are there any spiritual areas where you differ with your fiancée or spouse? Make a list, and begin to pray about these areas.

_____

_____

_____

_____

_____

10. List some of the ways you have shown your fiancée or spouse the love of Christ in the past few months.

a) _____

_____

_____

b) _____

_____

c) _____

_____

_____

d) _____

_____

_____

11. How can you love your wife as Christ loved the church? (See Ephesians 5:25-28.)

_____

_____

_____

_____

_____

12. What does it mean to dwell with your wife "with understanding" (1 Peter 3:7)?

_____

_____

_____

_____

_____

13. Are you aware of the likes and dislikes of your fiancée or spouse? If so, name a few.

   a) Likes:

_____

_____

_____

_____

_____

_____

   b) Dislikes:

_____

_____

_____

_____

_____

14. What activities do you like to do together?

a) _____

b) _____

c) _____

d) _____

e) _____

15. What kind of *spiritual* activities do you do together?

a) _____

b) _____

c) _____

d) _____

e) _____

16. What does it mean to "respect" your husband? (See Ephesians 5:33.)

_____

_____

_____

_____

_____

Notes

Notes

CHAPTER 3

Kindness, Forgiveness and Love

Be Kind

We have heard many people say that communication is the key to marriage. Kay Smith, the wife of our pastor said, "Communication is not the key to marriage; kindness is the key to marriage." Her statement is so true because we can actually *talk* our way into a divorce! The way to have a blessed relationship is to be kind to one another. The Scriptures say, "Therefore, as the elect of God, holy and beloved, put on tender mercies, kindness, humbleness of mind, meekness, longsuffering; bearing with one another, and forgiving one another, if anyone has a complaint against another; even as Christ forgave you, so you also must do. But above all these things put on love, which is the bond of perfection" (Colossians 3:12-14). Let's look at the roles kindness, forgiveness, and love play in the marital relationship.

Paul instructed the church at Colosse regarding "putting on" the attributes of God. The Greek word for "put on" is *enduo*, which means to sink into a garment. Paul, in a sense, is telling them to be clothed with a heart of mercy, kindness, humility, meekness, and longsuffering. Married couples today particularly need to be kind to one another. Kindness is sadly lacking in so many relationships. After two people get married, they begin to take each other for granted, and they do not treat each other with kindness. The Bible says, "And be kind to one another, tenderhearted, forgiving one another, just as God in Christ also forgave you" (Ephesians 4:32). The only way we can have genuine kindness coming forth out of our lives is if we are born again by the Spirit of God. (See John 3:1-21.) We cannot exemplify any of these attributes for any length of time in our own strength. We need to walk in the Spirit, and allow God to work in and through us. (See Galatians 5:16-25.)

I exhort many couples in my office each week. When some of them interact with one another, I hear the use of harsh words, sarcasm, cutting remarks, and there is a lack of courtesy. We need to be kind in the words we use, and in the actions we display. Men, do we open the door for our fiancée or spouse? Do we use the words "please" and "thank you" with each other? We might exemplify this behavior during our engagement because we want to put our best foot forward, however this can tend to change after the wedding vows have been exchanged. We all know that actions speak louder than words, and we want to continue to treat our spouse with kindness, courtesy, and love.

We need to be different than the people in "the world." People who do not have the Lord Jesus in their lives may engage in physical and verbal abuse, profanity, nagging, and yelling in order to communicate. The Apostle Paul said:

> You are the temple of the living God. As God has said: "I will dwell in them and walk among them. I will be their God, and they shall be My people." Therefore "come out from among them and be separate, says the Lord." (2 Corinthians 6:16,17)

We as Christians need to be different in the way we conduct ourselves in our homes. It starts right now while you are engaged. We should want ungodly people to notice that there is something unique about our relationship as believers in the Lord Jesus Christ. Contrary to what we might think, people are watching us! Paul also said, "You are our epistle written in our hearts, *known and read by all men*" (2 Corinthians 3:2)[Emphasis mine]. We want people to be attracted to the Lord in us because of the way we treat each other. This is one way we can be witnesses for God in the world in which we live. (See Matthew 5:16.) If you are getting remarried, and you have children, the children are watching you as well. They want to see *how this new man treats my mommy,* or *how does this lady treat my dad?* Your friends, your family, and your co-workers are watching how you treat one another, and we need to exemplify Christ in our behavior.

Hindrances to Kindness

Is there anything in your life that might be hindering you from being kind, from having a heart of mercy, humility, or a spirit of longsuffering? We have to be on guard because there are worldly influences all around us. We need to take an assessment of what is creeping into our lives and our homes. What are we watching on television?

48

What books and magazines are we reading? What kind of music do we listen to? All of these areas can be subtle ways that the enemy can influence us, and thereby tear down our marriage. (See 1 Peter 5:8,9.) I am sure you have heard that phrase, *Garbage in, garbage out*. It just means that whatever we put in our hearts and minds will come out in some way, at some time. Another way of putting it is:

> Do not be deceived, God is not mocked; for whatever a man sows, that he will also reap. For he who sows to his flesh will of the flesh reap corruption, but he who sows to the Spirit will of the Spirit reap everlasting life. (Galatians 6:7,8)

We want to sow to the Spirit! If we do, we will reap the fruit in our lives, and our marriages will benefit greatly. (See Galatians 5:22,23.)

Another area that is so important is the kinds of people with whom we spend time. Do we have godly friends? It is important to cultivate godly relationships with other couples during the time of your engagement. One way you can do this is to first pray about it. Ask the Lord to bring couples into your path that you admire at church. Perhaps they have been walking with the Lord a little longer than you have, and can set an example for you. In the Old Testament there is a Scripture that says that Saul was accompanied by a band of men "whose hearts God had touched" (1 Samuel 10:26). Can you say you keep company with people whose hearts have been touched by God? It will certainly make a difference in your marriage, and in your walk with the Lord.

One way to make godly friends is to come early to church, and hang around afterward for a while. So many people complain about churches being so large that they cannot get to know anyone, and yet they attend only on Sunday morning. They come late to the services, and at the conclusion, they are the first people out of the parking lot! Spending time with Christians after the services at your church will benefit you greatly. You may find some couples with which to pray, and you may end up going out for coffee afterward. It really depends upon you. Are you willing to put yourself in a place where God can bless you? Hang around, and see what God will do! Solomon said that a man that wants friends "must himself be friendly" (Proverbs 18:24). Reach out at church; ask the person next to you for a prayer request. You never know how God will bless you and them!

Conversely, you may have accumulated some friendships at work, or in the world, that do not glorify God. Now that you are engaged, you need to lessen the time you spend in those relationships. You may say, "But I am trying to win them to Christ." Well, let me propose this question, "Are you bringing them closer to the Lord, or are they influencing you?" A man came to me recently, and told me how he had not used profanity since he had become a Christian, but because of spending too much time with a nonbeliever, he began using it again. Yes, we are called to share with nonbelievers, but not at the expense of spending so much time with them that they water down our witness. Who is influencing whom? The Bible says, "He who walks with wise men will be wise, but the companion of fools will be destroyed" (Proverbs 13:20). We need to spend most of our free time with friends who are like-minded, and who will draw us closer to the Lord.

There are so many Scriptures in the Bible regarding kindness. There is one in Proverbs about the virtuous woman. It says, "She opens her mouth with wisdom, and on her tongue is the law of kindness" (Proverbs 31:26). We all know that we can use our tongues to build up or destroy people. The Bible also says, "Every wise woman builds her house, but the foolish pulls it down with her hands" (Proverbs 14:1). We need to edify, or build each other up in our relationships. It is so easy to look at the weaknesses, the shortcomings, and the failings of each other. We all have areas that the Holy Spirit needs to change, but we do not want to begin our engagement, or continue in our marriage by pointing out the faults in each other. David said, "Set a guard, O LORD, over my mouth; keep watch over the door of my lips" (Psalm 141:3). In other words, "Watch over my tongue so that the things I say to my fiancée or spouse are encouraging and kind." What we need to remember as believers in the Lord Jesus Christ is that if we are Christians, we will want to be kind and loving. These are manifestations of the fruit of the Spirit, and the desire God has for all of His children.

Forgiveness

We need to be forgiving toward one another. Four of the most important words we will use in marriage are, "Will you forgive me?" We should ask this question frequently of our spouse. I have talked to couples who are not willing to forgive one another, and they are doing so in direct contradiction to the Scriptures. The Bible says:

> Then Peter came to [Jesus] and said, "Lord, how often shall my brother sin against me, and I forgive him? Up to seven times?" Jesus said to him, "I do not say to you, up to seven times, but up to seventy times seven." (Matthew 18:21,22)

What we learn from this Scripture is that we are to forgive when we are asked, and that we are not to keep a record of the times we forgive. Many couples have shared with me that they have had difficulty being obedient to this Scripture. After their spouse has confessed their fault, and has asked forgiveness, they have said, "I do not feel like forgiving you right now. Let's talk about it in a few days." This is not acceptable. Paul said:

> And be kind to one another, tenderhearted, forgiving one another, *just as God in Christ also forgave you.* (Ephesians 4:32)[Emphasis mine.]

Jesus also mentioned this command in what is known as *The Lord's Prayer.* He said, "And forgive us our debts, as we forgive our debtors" (Matthew 6:12). We are to forgive whether we feel like it, or not! The Lord forgives us the moment we ask Him. He cleanses us, washes us, and we are restored into fellowship immediately. Two Scriptures from the Old and the New Testaments delineate this point:

> He will again have compassion on us, and will subdue our iniquities. You will cast all our sins into the depths of the sea. (Micah 7:19)

———

> And you, being dead in your trespasses and the uncircumcision of your flesh, He has made alive together with Him, having forgiven you all trespasses, having wiped out the handwriting of requirements that was against us, which was

contrary to us. And He has taken it out of the way, having
nailed it to the cross. (Colossians 2:13,14)

God knows all things, but He chooses not to hold our sins against us once we have asked forgiveness. He does not remind us of our past sins, and we should not do that with one another. He chastens those He loves, but He is always kind, tender, and forgiving when we confess to Him what we have done. (See Hebrews 12:5-11.)

To Forgive is to Forget

The Bible also says, "As far as the east is from the west, so far has He removed our transgressions from us" (Psalm 103:12). We need to treat each other the same way. If our fiancée or spouse has asked forgiveness, we should forgive them, and what they have done should be forgotten. There should be no sulking, or bitterness. I have heard people say, "I will forgive them because the Lord tells me I should, but I want to punish them as well. I want them to feel the pain of what they have done to me." Let me tell you: that is not forgiveness in the eyes of God. If we have truly forgiven, we will not hold a grudge, or try to make our fiancée or spouse suffer in any way after they have confessed their sin. We are not to keep a record of wrongs. We may say, "But you do not know what they have done to me!" That is not our concern, and we have to leave it in the hands of God. We will be the ones that suffer when we choose not to forgive.

God wants us to be well-balanced Christians, and He instructs us to forgive for our spiritual health. There are so many angry and bitter people in the world today because of a lack of forgiveness for others. We can actually sense the resentment in their attitude as they interact with individuals during the day. As Christians, we need to be different. We are to forgive as we have been forgiven, and we need to forgive others even if they have not asked. Remember what Jesus said on the cross when He died for our sins: "Father, forgive them, for they do not know what they do" (Luke 23:34). This is the type of attitude we are to have with one another: a love that not only forgives but would lay our very life down for the other. If we have truly forgiven our fiancée or spouse, we will not mention what they have done again, and this will restore joy to our relationship.

Running the Race Together

What a blessing it is to go through life with our best friend. I liken marriage to a three legged race at a picnic. In essence, we are running the race of Christianity side by side with the Lord Jesus at the finish line. Paul said in the Book of Hebrews:

> Therefore we also, since we are surrounded by so great a cloud of witnesses, let us lay aside every weight, and the sin which so easily ensnares us, and let us run with endurance the race that is set before us, looking unto Jesus, the author and finisher of our faith, who for the joy that was set before Him endured the cross, despising the shame, and has sat down at the right hand of the throne of God. (Hebrews 12:1,2)

In marriage we seek the Lord together through prayer, we attend church to further our understanding of the Word of God and His will for our lives, and we enjoy life by fellowshipping with other believers. Running this race together is so much fun!

In a real race, we would need to be looking straight ahead as we ran. If we look to our opponents on the left or the right, we may stumble. If we look back at who might be coming up behind us, we could lose our footing and fall. In the same way, we need to run the race of marriage by forgetting the past and the weaknesses of one another once they are confessed. If our "teammate" does not forgive, it is like being tied to a person who is carrying the past along with him like a ball and chain. How fast do you suppose we could run with a weight like that? The Lord wants us to forgive our spouse for past sins because it will only impede our progress.

The Story of Joseph

The story of Joseph is a great example of forgiveness. He was the second to the youngest of twelve brothers. His father, Jacob loved him because he was the son he had with Rachel, his first love. The Book of Genesis says:

> Now [Jacob] loved Joseph more than all his children, because he was the son of his old age. Also he made him a tunic of many colors. But when his brothers saw that their father loved him more than all his brothers, they hated him and could not speak peaceably to him. Now Joseph dreamed a dream, and he told it to his brothers; and they hated him even more. (Genesis 37:3-5)

Jacob probably made a mistake by favoring Joseph above the other children, and that exacerbated their jealousy toward him. Perhaps Joseph should not have shared the dreams he had with his brothers, but there is no doubt that they were prophetic dreams given to him by God. Joseph dreamed that he and his brothers were binding sheaves in the field; the sheaf of Joseph stood upright, and the other sheaves bowed down to it. After he shared his dreams with his father and brothers, the Scriptures say, "And his brothers envied him, but his father kept the matter in mind" (Genesis 37:11).

Later in the story, the sons of Jacob took their flocks to feed in Shechem. Jacob told Joseph to travel to where his brothers were, and to see how they fared. By the time he arrived in Shechem, they had moved to the city of Dothan. The Bible says:

> Now when they saw him afar off, even before he came near them, they conspired against him to kill him. Then they said to one another, "Look, this dreamer is coming! Come therefore, let us now kill him and cast him into some pit; and we shall say, 'Some wild beast has devoured him.' We shall see what will become of his dreams!" (Genesis 37:18-20)

The brothers did not kill him. They decided to make some money instead and sell him to a company of Ishmaelites who were traveling down to Egypt. The brothers took the special coat that Jacob had made for Joseph, and they dipped it in the blood of an animal. They told their father that they found the coat covered in blood, and assumed that wild beasts had devoured Joseph when he had come to look for them in Shechem. Jacob put on sackcloth, and mourned for his son for quite some time.

Joseph was sold to a man named Potiphar, and became his slave in Egypt for eleven years. Potiphar saw that God was with Joseph, and that He had allowed him to prosper. The Word of God says:

> So Joseph found favor in his sight, and served him. Then he made him overseer of his house, and all that he had he put in his hand. So it was, from the time that he had made him overseer of his house and all that he had, that the LORD blessed the Egyptian's house for Joseph's sake; and the blessing of the LORD was on all that he had in the house and in the field. (Genesis 39:4,5)

While he was a slave, he was falsely accused of trying to seduce the wife of Potiphar, and he spent two years in prison for this. While in prison, Joseph interpreted dreams that the baker and the butler had regarding their future service to the Pharaoh. After two years, Joseph was brought out of prison to interpret a dream the Pharaoh had regarding an ensuing seven-year famine. After Joseph interpreted the dream, he was placed as Prime Minister under Pharaoh in Egypt.

The famine arose in the land, and Joseph devised a plan to store up enough grain for Egypt and the surrounding areas for the seven years. Egypt was the only country that had grain for sale, so the sons of Jacob had to travel there in order to purchase the grain to feed their families. They had to meet with Joseph because he was in charge of the granaries, but they did not recognize him as their brother. This was due to the fact that they had not seen him in thirteen years, he was dressed in Egyptian clothing, and he spoke to them through an interpreter.

They went to buy grain two separate times, and Joseph revealed his identity to them on their second visit. The Scriptures say:

And Joseph said to his brothers, "Please come near to me." And they came near. And he said: "I am Joseph your brother, whom you sold into Egypt. But now, do not therefore be grieved or angry with yourselves because you sold me here; for God sent me before you to preserve life. So now it was not you who sent me here, but God; and He has made me a father to Pharaoh, and lord of all his house, and a ruler throughout all the land of Egypt." (Genesis 45:4,5,8)

What a story of forgiveness! After all his brothers did to him, Joseph could have said to himself, "There is a famine, and I am second in command in the land. My brothers will have to come down here to Egypt in order to buy grain, and when they do, I am going to get even with them for all they did to me." He did not say that at all. He forgave his brothers, and encouraged them that God was behind all that happened to him. Joseph was a living example of Romans 8:28 that says, "And we know that all things work together for good to those who love God, to those who are the called according to His purpose." He did not become angry or bitter at his brothers, and he did not try to retaliate in any way.

The story of Joseph is an example to us as well. He showed forgiveness to his brothers when they did not deserve it, and he forgave them in the spirit of gentleness. He did not chide them or become sarcastic, which we can do at times. Paul, the apostle said:

Brethren, if a man is overtaken in any trespass, you who are spiritual restore such a one in a spirit of gentleness, considering yourself lest you also be tempted. Bear one another's burdens, and so fulfill the law of Christ. (Galatians 6:1,2)

He could have been so disappointed that his own flesh and blood would sell him into slavery, and then lie about him to the father who loved him so dearly. But, he foreshadowed Jesus Christ by extending grace to them instead of judgement.

We do not deserve the forgiveness we have received from God. We need to extend mercy and forgiveness to each other as well. There will be times when we will be disappointed in our fiancée or our spouse. I know that sounds impossible if we are engaged, or newly married. We seem to have stars in our eyes, and everything is wonderful. There will come a time, however, when reality will set in for each of us. We will be disappointed in a decision, an attitude, or a reaction of the one we love. When this happens, we will feel let down, but God wants us to forgive. We need to say with the Apostle Paul:

> Being confident of this very thing, that He who has begun a
> good work in you will complete it until the day of Jesus Christ.
> (Philippians 1:6)

We need to believe the best about our fiancée or spouse. Just as God worked in the life of Joseph, He can work out something beautiful in our lives as we yield to Him. He can give us "beauty for ashes" in those areas where it has been difficult to forgive. (See Isaiah 61:3.) He is the God of restoration, and He can give us the strength to forgive and go on as if nothing had ever happened.

Love One Another

Love is the most important concept in the Bible. It is the love of God that brings us out of sin and into a relationship with Jesus Christ. God said to Jeremiah, the prophet:

> The LORD has appeared of old to me, saying: "Yes, I have
> loved you with an everlasting love; therefore with
> lovingkindness I have drawn you." (Jeremiah 31:3)

We also are familiar with one of the most wonderful verses in the Bible, and one that we probably all have memorized:

> For God so loved the world that He gave His only begotten

Son, that whoever believes in Him should not perish but have everlasting life. (John 3:16)

We are to love God, and we are to love one another. There are several words in the Greek language for the word love. There is *phileo* which is the love we would have for a friend. There is also *eros* which is a romantic, sexual, or worldly love. The type of love that God wants us to exemplify in marriage is *agape*. This is the type of love we mentioned earlier that we are supposed to "put on" according to the Apostle Paul in Colossians 3:12-14. The characteristics of *agape* are listed in 1 Corinthians 13. Paul says:

> Though I speak with the tongues of men and of angels, but have not love, I have become as sounding brass or a clanging cymbal. And though I have the gift of prophecy, and understand all mysteries and all knowledge, and though I have all faith, so that I could remove mountains, but have not love, I am nothing. And though I bestow all my goods to feed the poor, and though I give my body to be burned, but have not love, it profits me nothing. Love suffers long and is kind; love does not envy; love does not parade itself, is not puffed up; does not behave rudely, does not seek its own, is not provoked, thinks no evil; does not rejoice in iniquity, but rejoices in the truth; bears all things, believes all things, hopes all things, endures all things: Love never fails. (1 Corinthians 13:1-8)

If we do not have love, we are nothing. Do we love our fiancée or spouse in this way? This kind of love is self-sacrificing, it is kind, it does not envy, it is never rude, and it does not seek its own way. This unconditional love is the "bond of perfection," or the glue that holds our marriages together.

We responded to the Lord because of His kindness, forgiveness, and love. We are to "put on" these characteristics that we might have the peace of God in our homes. We cannot accomplish this in our own strength; we need the help of the Lord to live it out through us. But if we do exemplify these characteristics in our relationship, it will open the doors of communication, and it will make our marriage a light in the darkness that is all around us.

Review Questions

Kindness, Forgiveness, and Love

1. What sets us apart from the world? (See 2 Corinthians 6:17,18.)

_____

_____

_____

_____

_____

2. Has anything from the world crept into your life, or your relationship that could hinder your growth with the Lord, and with one another?

_____

_____

_____

_____

_____

3. Define the word *kindness*. (See Ephesians 4:32.)

_____

_____

_____

_____

_____

4. "Every wise woman builds her house" (Proverbs 14:1). List some ways that you can build your home.

a) _____

b) _____

c) _____

d) _____

e) _____

5. What does it mean to love someone with *agape* love? (See 1 Corinthians 13.)

_____

_____

_____

_____

_____

6. Do you find agape love in your relationship today? Briefly describe a recent example.

_____

_____

_____

_____

_____

7. What does it mean to forgive? List one Scripture that validates your answer.

_____

_____

_____

_____

_____

8. Have you had to forgive your fiancée or spouse recently? When they confessed their sin or asked forgiveness, what was your response?

_____

_____

_____

_____

_____

9. Read Philippians 3:13,14. Why is it important to forget the past?

_____

_____

_____

_____

_____

10. Do you tend to hold on to the problems of the past? List some suggestions from Philippians, or other Scriptures that will help you overcome this tendency.

_____

_____

_____

_____

_____

11. What does it mean to "Bear one another's burdens"? (See Galatians 6:1,2.)

_____

_____

_____

_____

_____

Notes

Notes

CHAPTER 4

Communication

Walk in the Spirit

We need to have good communication skills in order to have a strong and successful marriage. There are some things only God can do, but we also have responsibilities to fulfill as Christians. One of the most important things we can do to build our communication is to walk in the Spirit. The Bible says:

> Walk in the Spirit, and you shall not fulfill the lust of the flesh. For the flesh lusts against the Spirit, and the Spirit against the flesh; and these are contrary to one another, so that you do not do the things that you wish. (Galatians 5:16,17)

If we are walking in the Spirit, there will be the fruit of the Spirit evident in our lives: "love, joy, peace, longsuffering, kindness, goodness, faithfulness, gentleness, self-control" (Galatians 5:22,23). These are definitely catalysts for successful communication with one another!

There are also certain steps we can take to help us walk in the Spirit. One is to read the Word of God on a daily basis. As we read the Bible, it gives us new direction in our lives. It puts the desires of God in our hearts, rather than what we think we should accomplish. (See Psalm 37:4 and Philippians 2:13.) I used to teach Sunday School several years ago, and I remember coming across a page for the children to color. It said, "Seven days without God's Word makes one weak." What a true statement! The Bible is our lifeline with God.

To help us walk in the Spirit, we also need to pray on a regular basis. Paul said, "Pray without ceasing" (1 Thessalonians 5:17). Solomon also said:

> Trust in the LORD with all your heart, and lean not on your own understanding; in all our ways acknowledge Him, and He shall direct your paths. (Proverbs 3:5,6)

Reading the Word and praying are basic things we need to do together as husbands and wives. I have heard wonderful stories of couples having prayer meetings together weekly, or calling each other at night to read the Bible and pray over the phone before they got married. These are great habits to start! Conversely, I have heard of couples who pray together while they are engaged, and then as soon as they are married, they stop because of the pressures of life. We need to continue in the things of God. Reading the Word and praying on a regular basis will help us walk in the Spirit, and thus become better communicators.

It is so easy to say, "I am not a good communicator, and I never will be." But God can help us learn to communicate. It is something we need to develop, and we begin by spending as much time as we can together just talking. Ask questions, and find out about the person you are marrying. You can never spend too much time talking over coffee, taking long walks, and spending time in prayer with one another, asking God to show you more about your fiancée or spouse.

Encourage One Another

We also want to be people who edify, or build up one another, because this is what the Bible instructs us to do. If we think of ourselves as builders, we will want to say and do those things that will encourage and strengthen our relationship as a couple. The Apostle Paul said:

> Therefore, putting away lying, each one speak truth with his neighbor, for we are members of one another. "Be angry, and do not sin": do not let the sun go down on your wrath, nor give place to the devil. Let him who stole steal no longer, but rather let him labor, working with his hands what is good, that he may have something to give him who has need. Let no corrupt communication proceed out of your mouth, but what is good for necessary edification, that it may impart grace to the hearers. And do not grieve the Holy Spirit of God, by

whom you were sealed for the day of redemption. Let all bitterness, wrath, anger, clamor, and evil speaking be put away from you, with all malice. And be kind to one another, tenderhearted, forgiving one another, just as God in Christ also forgave you. (Ephesians 4:25-32)

He also said, "Let your speech always be with grace, seasoned with salt, that you may know how you ought to answer each one" (Colossians 4:6). What we say should always build up others. It is so easy to give in to the flesh life, and say unkind and cutting things to the ones we love. But this is not what God wants for our relationships. Paul said, "Let your speech always be...seasoned with salt." What does salt do? It preserves and heals. We want to make sure our words do not destroy, but that they are used to bring healing to the lives of others.

We all agree that "out in the world" we can get torn down as Christians. People who do not have Jesus Christ in their lives oftentimes have little regard for the feelings of others. They gossip and say unkind things behind the backs, and even to the faces of individuals. How often do we get a pat on the back for doing a good job at work? It is rare, if we receive one at all! But if a project we have been working on fails to some degree, we will hear about it right away – that is practically a guarantee! This should not be a characteristic in our marriages, or in the body of Christ at large. We need to be encouraging to one another. The Lord certainly is encouraging to us, and we need to follow His example.

Let's ask ourselves these questions:

• Do we look for the good in others?

• Does our conversation primarily center on ourselves, or do we try to relate to, and encourage others?

• Do we build up, tear down, or nag when we speak to people?

• When we do not get our way, do we become angry?

Solomon said, "Death and life are in the power of the tongue, and those who love it will eat its fruit" (Proverbs 18:21). It is amazing to think that we can destroy, or bring life and encouragement by the things we say. Jesus said, "If a house is divided against itself, that house cannot stand" (Mark 3:25). We can provide a great foundation for our future home by communicating love and healing before we even get to the altar. Proverbs 15:1 says, "A soft answer turns away wrath, but a harsh word stirs up anger." This is a Scripture that we memorized together before we got married. We told each other that we would make our best effort not to raise our voices in our home. We have had disagreements in the past twenty years like any couple, but memorizing that Proverb has helped us calmly resolve our differences.

Let's liken the concept of encouragement in marriage to building a custom home. Rynner and I came home a few months ago, and found a set of blueprints at our door that had been misdirected. We unrolled the prints in order to look for a company name so we could notify them of their delivery error. In examining them we saw that they were plans for a 30,000 square foot home. We were amazed. There were eight or ten bedrooms, several bathrooms, a library, a sauna, a weight room, a music room, a conservatory, quarters for the maids, and so on. This was obviously the dream home that someone was going to build. After we had put the blueprints away we began to ponder the time and energy it would take for such a project. We would have ideas of what we wanted; we then would share them with the architect. After several weeks of decisions and changes, he would draw up blueprints of what we desired. They would then be submitted to the various city departments. Once the plans were approved, the actual building would begin. There would be men who would frame the house, others would put up the drywall; plumbers, electricians, glass men, and painters would work for weeks, or even months. When the home is finished, there would be all of the decisions regarding the decorating of the home. Should we have carpet or hard wood floors? What style of furniture and window dressings shall we choose? Do we want marble countertops for the kitchen, or tile? What type of knobs shall we have for the cabinets? Building a custom home is a tremendous undertaking of time, patience, and resources! It could take a year or more from start to finish to complete this home. This is what is involved when it comes to building.

Now imagine that we were going to demolish this home once it is finished. We call the company with a wrecking ball, and in fifteen minutes our home is flattened to the ground. Do we see the similarity in regard to our tongues? It can take years to build a great relationship with our spouse, and one hurtful comment can hurt us and stay with us for a lifetime. Whenever we become angry, we say things we regret. We do not want to use our tongues to tear down, but to edify, build and encourage.

How Do We Communicate?

There are two ways to communicate: verbally and nonverbally. What is nonverbal communication? A few examples would be a shrug of the shoulders, a wink, a touch of the hand, a smile, a hug, or a kiss. There are specific ways of communicating nonverbally. A man told me that when he was upset, he would look at his wife with one eyebrow raised. When she saw that eyebrow, she knew that she was in trouble. He was not using any words, but he was definitely communicating something to her!

There are many levels of communication, from the very basic of "how are you" to the deeper level of sharing your fears, struggles, and goals with each other. This is the depth of communication that we all should desire in our marriages. Oddly enough, some married couples never get to this level! I have talked to many couples who have had problems in this area because of fear. They feel if they share what they have done in the past, their current fears, or how they really feel about something, they will be rejected by their fiancée or spouse.

Another reason could be that we just will not take the time to express our true feelings. Our schedules can be so hectic. You and your fiancée are probably both working, and/or going to school; you may even live in different cities! All of these things crowd out our time with one another. Just remember that it takes trust to get to this deeper level of sharing, and it takes time to build trust. We need to guard our time, and set up "date nights" even after we get married to ensure that we are maintaining this level of communication.

I think it is more difficult for men to get to the point of sharing deeply than it is for women. The reason for this probably has something to do with our society. Somehow, men have developed a need to show others that they are not weak or needy in any area. Being candid and open with people about our weaknesses might give people the impression that we do not have it all together. Of course, we know that this involves pride, and we want to guard against this. Pride is sin, and it will keep us from experiencing the depth of relationship that God wants us to have with our spouse. (See Proverbs 6:16-19 and Proverbs 8:13.)

Listening

Do you know the fears of your fiancée or spouse? Have you ever asked them? Do you take the time to listen when they do share with you? On a scale from one to ten, how would you rate your listening skills? Would you say that you are a good listener? We cannot stress the importance of listening in relation to communication. James said:

> Therefore, my beloved brethren, let every man be *swift to hear*, slow to speak, slow to wrath; for the wrath of man does not produce the righteousness of God. (James 1:19,20)[Emphasis mine.]

We cannot develop much of a relationship with anyone if we are always doing the talking. When we listen, we find out all kinds of things. We want to get to the place where we are open, where nothing is hidden, and we are sharing everything. If we are not keeping anything from our fiancée or spouse, we will be much more apt to share our fears, goals, and hopes we have for our future.

We need to ask ourselves, do we really listen to one another? This is something we all need to work on continually, because it always seems to be a challenge. We need to listen with both ears as well, not just with one ear, if you know what I mean. If your fiancée or spouse is trying to share something with you, are you looking at the television? Is your face in the newspaper, or are you working on a project? One woman shared with me that whenever her husband was home, the television was always on. She became so frustrated that she told him she was tired of trying to communicate with him over the din of a football game. She said, "Now he mutes the television while she is talking, but his eyes are still watching the game!" That is not God's ideal. Was her husband really listening to all she was saying? Oh, he may have heard a word now and then about "school clothes for the kids," or something about "the car needing oil" but that was probably about all he could have repeated to you. What was he communicating to his wife while she was talking? He was communicating to her that he did not really think that what she had to say was important. We listen to people we respect. Was he showing his wife respect by listening to her with one ear while his other ear, and all of his concentration, was on a football game? Would he listen to his boss at work this way? Would this husband have looked another way as his superior explained an upcoming project and thought, "Yeah, yeah, yeah, I will get it done"? Of course not. He could get fired! I think this wife would have probably passed out if this man had turned off the television, and if he would have put his arm around her and said, "Honey, tell me all about it. What is on your mind, and how can I help you?" Now, that would have been giving her his full attention. Giving our fiancée or spouse our full attention shows that they are important to us.

Now, it should be noted that statistically, women speak 25,000 words in an average day, as opposed to men who speak 12,000 words. This can become a challenge for both of us. Men, are we listening to our fiancée or spouse with our full concentration while she is talking? Women, are we wise in choosing the times we select to discuss important issues? For example, this wife could have prayed, "Lord, what would be a good time for me to talk to Bob about school clothes for the kids?" Now, she knows it is football season, and that Bob is a die-hard Packer fan. His team is in the playoffs. If they make this field goal against the Chicago Bears, Wisconsin will win by one point. The Lord is definitely not going to tell Debbie to discuss school clothes with Bob at this crucial moment! We need to be sensitive to each other.

God tells men in the New Testament:

> Likewise you husbands, dwell with [your wives] with understanding, giving honor to the wife, as to the weaker vessel, and as being heirs together of the grace of life, that your prayers may not be hindered. (1 Peter 3:7)

That word "understanding" means to investigate. Men, we are to be an investigator in order to understand our wives physically, emotionally, and spiritually. Husbands need to be aware of what is going on in the household. When we think of a good investigator, what is one of the most important skills necessary to find the clues to solve a crime? We need to ask questions, and we need to listen! As we do this, we will gain insight concerning the spiritual, physical, and emotional state of our wife. This will not only encourage them, but will help to promote healthy communication.

Hindrances to Communication

As Christians, we still have to deal with the flesh life. The works of the flesh will cause difficulty in our communication if we continue in them. Paul lists a few of them in the Book of Colossians:

> But now you must also put off all these: anger, wrath, malice, blasphemy, filthy language out of your mouth. Do not lie to one to another, since you have put off the old man with his deeds, and have put on the new man who is renewed in knowledge according to the image of Him who created him. (Colossians 3:8-10)

We are to "put off the old man." Anger, wrath, malice, lying, and filthy language will hinder the growth of our relationship.

What is Our Attitude?

What is our attitude toward one another when we are communicating? When our fiancée or spouse addresses us concerning an area of weakness in our lives, or if they are concerned about us in some way, are we proud and arrogant? Remember, "God resists the proud, but gives grace to the humble" (James 4:6). We need to ask ourselves some questions that will assess what kind of communicator we are:

• What kind of words do we use when we talk to each other?

• Do we use harsh tones?

- Are we critical?

- Are we condemning?

- Do we try to justify our actions, or our sin?

- Do we have a propensity to tear down, nag, or point fingers?

- Do we exaggerate or lie?

- Do we use foul language?

Paul said that we are to put off all these things. If we do not, our communication with each other will be hindered.

Not Telling the Truth

I recently talked to a couple, and the wife shared with me that her husband was a chronic liar. She felt that she could not trust him regarding anything he was telling her, because he never told the truth, even in small, insignificant areas. This obviously hindered their communication. It had built up a wall between them, and they had eventually stopped talking to each other!

We need to always tell the truth. Jesus said that Satan is the father of lies. (See John 8:44.) Paul said, "[Speak] the truth in love" (Ephesians 4:15). This command can be difficult. Our fiancée or spouse could ask us if we like the dress she is wearing, and we may not particularly care for it. If we want to tell the "truth in love," we could say, "I liked the one you had on yesterday much more than this one." As a woman, our fiancé or spouse could ask us how we thought he looked. Our first thought could be, "Is he colorblind?" Or "I wonder if he slept in those clothes." If we want to share the "truth in love" we could say, "Why don't you take off the plaid jacket for the night. It is kind of warm." Then later on suggest that you go shopping together so you can pick up a few basics for him. We, of course, want to make our comments in the most loving way we possibly can, so we do not hurt their feelings. These are small areas, but they are still important. If we do not have the victory in speaking the truth in the smaller areas of life, we most assuredly will struggle when the big issues arise.

Anger

Another hindrance to good communication is anger. What happens when a person raises their voice, or begins throwing objects? It evokes fear in the other person, and they will retaliate by getting angry themselves in defense of their position. Doors might slam, or one of the parties will end up leaving the house for a few hours. Anger causes division. Solomon said, "A soft answer turns away wrath, but a harsh word stirs up anger" (Proverbs 15:1). Many husbands and wives go to bed with anger or resentment in their hearts against their spouse, and this is not healthy for the relationship. The Bible says, " 'Be angry, and do not sin': do not let the sun go down on your wrath, nor give place to the devil" (Ephesians 4:26,27). This Scripture simply means that we are not to be angry, and we are not to go to sleep at night without resolving our differences with one another. If we do, we will be giving the devil a foothold in our marriage. We need to take the time to talk about how we feel without raised voices, or condemnation of each other. We need to be able to pray together without bitterness in our hearts before we go to sleep each evening.

If we are angry with one another, and we do not resolve the conflict, a wall can be erected between us. Each unresolved argument becomes a brick, and before long the wall is so tall that we cannot even see each other. When couples declare that they have fallen out of love, or that they just cannot communicate anymore, it is a result of many unresolved conflicts. A couple we knew was having difficulty communicating several years ago, when they were first married. The wife would try to share her feelings with her husband in a calm voice. He would proceed to turn it into an argument that became her fault every time. He would never take the blame because he was too full of pride to ever admit that he could be wrong. In frustration, she would lay her head back on the pillow in the darkness of their bedroom, and the tears would stream down her face. She did not want to make any sounds by crying, because even that would irritate him. This is not the way the Lord wants us to communicate with one another. We need to be able to have an open forum together. If you are at fault, own up to it. Each of you needs to express your side, acknowledge your weakness, and ask forgiveness. We all see situations differently, but we need to agree on some basics:

- We will not raise our voices.

- We should be able to express our opinions without being interrupted. (Try to limit each thought to a few minutes.)

- If we cannot agree, we need to talk to a pastor at our church who can be the intermediary. We need to be at peace with one another, and the Lord. (See 2 Corinthians 5:18.)

An important Scripture to remember is, "Husbands, love your wives and do not be bitter toward them" (Colossians 3:19). The enemy wants us to hold onto bitterness or anger because he knows he can destroy our communication through it. We need to guard against this because Peter said:

> Likewise you husbands, dwell with [your wives] with understanding, giving honor to the wife, as to the weaker vessel, and as being heirs together of the grace of life, that *your prayers may not be hindered.* (1 Peter 3:7)[Emphasis mine.]

If we become bitter against one another, it can actually impede the efficacy of our prayers. Isaiah said, "Behold, the LORD'S hand is not shortened, that it cannot save; nor His ear heavy, that it cannot hear. But your iniquities have separated you from your God; and your sins have hidden His face from you, so that He will not hear" (Isaiah 59:1,2). Do you see the importance of maintaining a clean slate before the Lord, and before one another? We need to be regularly discussing, and asking forgiveness for our shortcomings and sins, or they will hinder our prayer life, and our relationship with one another. Andy Rooney said, "I have learned that when you harbor bitterness, happiness will dock elsewhere." We do not want anger or bitterness to build a wall between us in our marriage, or to keep us from experiencing the joy of the Lord.

It is interesting that both Paul and Peter address the husbands in these two Scriptures. They write to the men specifically because, as I have stated before, we set the tone in our homes. The enemy will try to get to us first, because he knows that if he can get us to succumb to his tactics, the entire home can be brought to ruin. Our wives and children will follow our example, and we need to be aware of this. A friend we know grew up with a father who was angry all the time. He was not a Christian, and everyone in the family was on edge whenever he was home. They were all concerned about not upsetting their dad. He was a time bomb waiting to go off if he did not get his way. This involved yelling, profanity, and even throwing things on occasion. What kind of atmosphere do you think this created for his wife and children? They lived in a world of fear because this man was so immersed in himself. We need to pray that God will give us the victory over anger, and ask Him to remove it. He is the God of miracles.

Not Confessing Our Faults

Another hindrance to communication is an unwillingness to confess our faults. In Chapter One we discussed the importance of confession in our relationships, but it bears mentioning here as well. James said:

> Confess your trespasses to one another, and pray for one another, that you may be healed. The effective, fervent prayer of a righteous man avails much. (James 5:16)

What we do will affect others. If we sin against our spouse in some way, and we do not confess it to them, our relationship will be adversely affected. We will start to act quirky, and demonstrate abnormal behavior. We will become angry individuals because we are hiding things, and we will not be experiencing the abundant life that Christ has for us. (See John 10:10.) We need to take responsibility for our actions, and not transfer the blame onto others. When God confronted Adam in the Garden of Eden regarding his sin, Adam blamed Eve. She, in turn, blamed the serpent. (See Genesis 3:6-13.) It seems to be part of human nature to put the blame for our choices on others. I listen to couples weekly in my office, and on occasion they will attribute their weaknesses and propensities to sin in certain areas to their spouse. They say, "If she were more encouraging, I would not act this way," or "If he earned more money, I would not nag him so much." We even knew of a man a few years ago who said, "If my wife would lose weight, I would treat her differently." So, this wife took his words to heart. She joined a gym, and worked very hard to bring her five foot three frame down from about 250 pounds to 115 in about a year and a half. What do you think happened? He still treated her the same.

Another Christian man we knew used to drink a lot, sometimes even to the point of inebriation. He said, "I am getting older, and God has not brought me a mate, and I am lonely. Several years later, he got married to a sweet Christian girl, and he still drinks too much. One blamed his wife, and the other blamed his singleness. What was the real problem? These men were not satisfied with their relationships with Jesus Christ. Peter said, "His divine power has given to us all things that pertain to life and godliness" (2 Peter 1:3). These men were looking for fulfillment in the wrong place! We will never have true fulfillment in life outside of Jesus Christ. We cannot blame our circumstances or people for our behavior. We have to take responsibility for our own actions. We need to confess our faults to one another, and ask forgiveness. We have to come together in prayer, and ask the Lord for victory in our areas of weakness. Remember "The effective, fervent prayer of a righteous man avails much" (James 5:16).

Review Questions

Communication

Meditate on the Psalm below and pray before answering the following questions.

"Search me, O God, and know my heart; try me, and know my anxieties; and see if there is any wicked way in me, and lead me in the way everlasting" (Psalm 139:23,24).

1. What does it mean to edify?

    _____
    _____
    _____
    _____
    _____

2. Think about how you communicate with your fiancée or spouse. Would you categorize yourself as a builder? List some ways in which you can build up one another.

    a) _____
    b) _____
    c) _____
    d) _____
    e) _____

3. List some nonverbal ways in which you communicate with your fiancée or spouse. Next, list some nonverbal ways they communicate with you. After you have done this, write what your nonverbal communication means to your fiancée

or spouse, and what their nonverbal communication means to you. Compare and discuss your responses.

_____

_____

_____

_____

_____

4. Listening is a vital part of communication. On a scale from 1-10, how would you rate your listening skills? How would you rate those of your fiancée or spouse?

_____

_____

_____

_____

_____

5. Why do you think the Lord tells us to be "swift to hear" (James 1:19)?

_____

_____

_____

_____

_____

6. How can you tell when your fiancée or spouse is listening to you?

_____

_____

_____

_____

_____

7. Make a list of things that have hindered your communication.

a) _____

b) _____

c) _____

d) _____

8. What is your attitude when you communicate with others?

_____

_____

_____

_____

_____

9. If you tend to be critical, judgmental, or abusive in your communication, to what would you attribute this?

_____

_____

_____

_____

_____

10. Make a list of things that encourage good communication.

a) _____

b) _____

c) _____

d) _____

e) _____

11. What does it mean to "Walk in the Spirit"? (See Galatians 5:16-26.)

_____

_____

_____

_____

_____

12. List some practical ways in which you can walk in the Spirit.

a) _____

b) _____

c) _____

d) _____

e) _____

Notes

Notes

_____

_____

_____

_____

_____

_____

_____

_____

_____

_____

_____

_____

_____

_____

_____

_____

_____

_____

_____

_____

_____

_____

_____

CHAPTER FIVE

Resolving Conflict

Conflict in the Bible

Have you and your fiancée had any conflicts since you have become engaged? I think the greatest conflicts my wife and I experienced occurred during our engagement period. I think the enemy tries to destroy our relationships before we even get to the altar! If he can destroy marriages, he can potentially destroy a nation.

From the beginning of time, man has had conflict. There are many examples in the Bible regarding conflict: Abraham and Sarah, Isaac and Rebekah, Jacob and Rachel, and David and Michal, to name a few. Conflict in our relationships is inevitable, but how do we handle it when it arises? The Early Church in the Book of Acts dealt with conflict, and had great results. The Bible says:

> Now in those days, when the number of the disciples was multiplying, there arose a murmuring against the Hebrews by the Hellenists, because their widows were neglected in the daily distribution [of food]. Then the twelve summoned the multitude of the disciples and said, "It is not desirable that we should leave the word of God and serve tables. Therefore, brethren, seek out from among you seven men of good reputation, full of the Holy Spirit and wisdom, whom we may appoint over this business; but we will give ourselves continually to prayer and to the ministry of the word." And the saying pleased the whole multitude. And the word of God spread, and the number of the disciples multiplied greatly in Jerusalem. (Acts 6:1-5,7)

The church began to grow rapidly, and there were complaints from the Grecian Jews that there was discrimination against the widows in their community. They felt they were not given as much food in the daily distribution as the widows that spoke Hebrew. The twelve apostles decided to call a meeting of all the believers. They felt that they should spend their time studying the Word of God and in prayer, rather than feeding the poor. We know that if the pastor is involved with too many secondary tasks, he will neglect the most important aspect of his ministry. Thus, the apostles selected seven men in the fellowship with a good reputation who would be in charge of the distribution of food in order that everyone would receive their fair share.

We can see that God worked in the Early Church in a mighty way, and the Word of God increased. In spite of what we may think, conflict can actually be good at times! They had a problem, and the Lord gave to them the wisdom to solve it. Warren Wiersbe said:

> When a church [or in our case a marriage], faces a serious problem, this presents the leaders [or the spouses] with a number of opportunities. For one thing, problems give us the opportunity to examine our ministry [or marriage] and discover what changes must be made. We must regularly examine our lives and our ministries lest we start taking things for granted.[3]

We do not want to take each other for granted. Conflict can be a blessing, but only if we use it constructively to help us get to know each other better.

There were also certain attributes that the Early Church possessed that turned this stumbling block into a stepping stone. First, the people had a heart to serve the Lord. In other words, this fellowship was not full of self-seeking individuals. They had a common goal. If we want to stay married our goal must always be to resolve our differences. We cannot always have our own way. We both need to yield to our desires at times in order to reach common ground, and to resolve conflict.

Warren Wiersbe also said:

> The apostles studied the situation and concluded that *they* were to blame: they were so busy serving tables [for the distribution of food] that they were neglecting prayer and the ministry of the Word of God. They had created their own problem because they were trying to do too much.[4]

What can we conclude from this? The leaders of the fellowship were not ashamed to admit that they had made a mistake, and that they wanted to correct it. What an example the resolution of this conflict is for our marriages! We as husbands and leaders have to be able to confess our shortcomings when we have erred. We need to set the example of humility in the home. What difference does it make if we have made an incorrect choice? We are all human; we make mistakes. We all sin before the Lord and each other. To think that we are infallible as a husband or a wife is ridiculous! We sin because we are sinners, and that is just a part of life. (See Romans 3:23.) But what do we do when we fail? Do we yell and scream? Do we try to foist the blame on others to take the pressure off of ourselves? We need to take ownership for what we have done. We need to confess our faults and as a result, our wives and family members will follow our lead.

We also know that the Early Church was a body of believers that prayed. As we ask the Lord for direction when conflicts arise, He will give us wisdom. (See James 1:5.) When we have a disagreement, it is so important that someone initiates reconciliation through prayer. The Lord only needs one willing party! The Bible says:

> Now all things are of God, who has reconciled us to Himself through Jesus Christ, and has given us the ministry of reconciliation. (2 Corinthians 5:18)

We all have the ministry of reconciliation if we are Christians, and we are to be at peace with God, and with one another. Jesus said, "Blessed are the peacemakers, for they shall be called sons of God" (Matthew 5:9). It is a challenge to be a peacemaker. When we were newlyweds, I remember a specific time when I would not forgive Rynner for a simple infraction. I was so immature, and it is humbling for me to even express it. Solomon said, "By pride comes only contention, but with the well-advised is wisdom" (Proverbs 13:10), and "He who is of a proud heart stirs up strife, but he who trusts in the LORD will be prospered" (Proverbs 28:25). Pride is sin, and it will keep us from the ministry of reconciliation.

A few other attitudes that will keep us polarized are anger, strife, criticism, pointing fingers, alcohol, substance abuse, or pornography. Anything of the flesh life will bring conflict into our relationships. (See Galatians 5:19-21.) We can try to put it out of our minds for a time, or sweep it under the carpet, but it will continue to surface. There will be problems regarding that sin, or that attitude, and we need to resolve them. The Lord worked in a wonderful way in the Early Church, and people came to know Him through their witness because they were at peace with one another. When conflict is resolved between us, and we have peace in our relationship, what an impact we can have in the lives of others.

How to Resolve Conflict

In order to resolve conflict, we first need to be willing. God can begin to work, as I said, even if only one of us is open to bringing about reconciliation. Solomon said, "When a man's ways please the LORD, He makes even his enemies to be at peace with him" (Proverbs 16:7). That is a powerful Scripture! If we are pursuing the things of God, and putting Him first, God can change the heart of our spouse, and make them at peace with us.

When there is conflict, and the tempers are raging, we need to take action quickly. The longer we wait, the more difficult it becomes to resolve our problems. Time distorts the facts, and to say, "Six weeks ago, you said...." is not the ideal. We need to take action right away. Remember Paul said, "Do not let the sun go down on your wrath" (Ephesians 4:26). That means we need to resolve the problem now, and not go to sleep with anger in our hearts toward one another. Jesus said:

> Therefore if you bring your gift to the altar, and there remember that your brother has something against you, leave your gift there before the altar, and go your way. First be reconciled to your brother [or your spouse], and then come and offer your gift. (Matthew 5:23,24)

A couple could be having a disagreement on a Saturday afternoon, and they go to sleep Saturday night without coming to a resolution. They drive to church on Sunday morning without speaking to one another. But while they are in the sanctuary, they smile at their friends, and act as if nothing is wrong. They lift their hands in praise to the Lord during worship, and then they drive home without speaking because they have not resolved their conflict. There is definitely something wrong with this picture! Jesus is saying that we should resolve our conflicts first, and then go into church to worship Him.

Be Honest With One Another

We can also resolve conflict more quickly by being completely honest with one another. King David was not honest after he had committed adultery with Bathsheba. When Bathsheba sent word to David that she was pregnant, he proceeded to cover his sin by having Uriah, her husband sent home from the battle that Israel was fighting. David hoped that Uriah would have conjugal relations with his wife, and David would not be discovered as the father of the child. Uriah refused to go down to his house saying:

> The ark and Israel and Judah are dwelling in tents, and my lord Joab and the servants of my lord are encamped in the open fields. Shall I then go to my house to eat and drink, and to lie with my wife? As you live, and as your soul lives, I will not do this thing. (2 Samuel 11:11)

Uriah thwarted the plan of David by having such a strong character. Because of this, David sent word to Joab to put Uriah into the heat of the battle so that he would be killed. Uriah was killed, and David took Bathsheba into his palace to be his wife. The Bible says, "But the thing that David had done displeased the LORD" (2 Samuel 11:27). David attempted to cover his sin, and he was not being honest with himself or with others in regard to what really happened. Solomon said, "He who covers his sins will not prosper, but whoever confesses and forsakes them will have mercy" (Proverbs 28:13). We need to be honest with one another. There will not be reconciliation if we try to hide from one another regarding our faults and sins.

Attack the Problem, Not Each Other

We do not want to run from our problems. I was praying with a man who had a disagreement with his wife, and he refused to confront the situation. He did not want to go into his house after work when he saw his wife's car parked in the driveway that day. He said, "Going into that house *means strife* to me!" When conflict arises, we should not retreat. We need to pray and ask the Lord, "What is causing the problem?" We do not want to retreat; we want to attack the problem, and not each other.

If there is a difficulty with finances, alcohol, drugs, or even something small like a husband not coming home on time, we need to get to the root of the problem, and not begin to yell, or point fingers. Pastor Steve Carr shares a story about a husband who was never on time.

> Years ago, a couple came to me very angry with each other, asking my counsel over a problem. It began when the husband didn't come home from work one evening. His wife had dinner ready that night, and expected him at six o'clock, his usual time of arrival. The kids were waiting and everyone was hungry for dinner, but Dad didn't show up. The mother and kids finally ate dinner at about seven-thirty without Dad. He came home at about eight o'clock expecting everything to be normal. Needless to say, his wife was a little upset when he walked through the door. The two had a heated exchange of words, then reconciled later that night. The husband explained that he had been out with some of the men from work. He asked her forgiveness, and they kissed and made up. The wife wasn't upset he had gone out, only that he didn't let her know he would be late.
>
> A few weeks later the same thing happened again, only this time his wife was very angry. They reconciled again and all

94

was well until one Saturday afternoon when the husband failed to come home after going to the hardware store. He was gone the whole day. The husband just seemed to always get sidetracked and would fail to call. Each time he asked for forgiveness, but he continued the offensive behavior. Their relationship became very strained, and they decided to come for counseling.

I explained to them that they had reconciled the conflict every time, but they had not solved the problem. What they needed to do was to set up a practical plan to keep the problem from happening again. Failure to devise a plan only guaranteed future conflicts.

I gave them a number of possible solutions; one of which was for the husband to *call* if he was going to be more than a half an hour late. Second, he wasn't in the habit of wearing a watch, which contributed to his losing track of time, so I asked him to purchase one. Finally, I also encouraged him to stick a note to his dashboard as a reminder of his responsibility to call his wife.

This solution worked very well. They came back months later to tell me that there had not been one problem since our appointment. Why? Because they fully resolved the problem! They took creative and practical steps to keep it from ever happening again.[5]

David said, "Search me, O God, and know my heart; try me, and know my anxieties; and see if there is any wicked way in me, and lead me in the way everlasting" (Psalm 139:23,24). We need to pray, "Lord, am I the cause of any conflict in our relationship? Help me to be a minister of reconciliation." Once we have prayed that prayer, God will show us the areas where we need to work to find a solution. In the Book of Acts, there was contention between the Hellenists and the Hebrews. The apostles pinpointed the problem, and proposed a solution. The multitude was pleased, and it brought forth peace.

We want our homes to be a sanctuary from the world, and a place where we can rest. Who wants to come home from a hard day, and start fighting with their spouse? Let's take these truths and begin to apply them to our relationship today. The Lord will help us get the victory as we do our part, and the end result will be peace.

Spiritual Warfare

We need to realize that we may also be experiencing conflict because we are being attacked by the devil. The Scriptures say, "Be sober, be vigilant; because your adversary the devil walks about like a roaring lion, seeking whom he may devour" (1 Peter 5:8). Jesus spoke to Peter about this when He said, "Simon, Simon! Indeed, Satan has asked for you, that he may sift you as wheat. But I have prayed for you, that your faith should not fail" (Luke 22:31,32). Jesus acknowledged that there is a devil, and that he wants to sift all of us like wheat. We may be in a heated argument in our marriage, and we fail to recognize that it is the enemy who is stirring up the disagreement between us. The fact is, we are in a spiritual battle. This is demonstrated by the fact that Paul the apostle refers to us as soldiers in the New Testament. He reminded Timothy of this when he said:

> You therefore must endure hardship as a good soldier of Jesus Christ. No one engaged in warfare entangles himself with the affairs of this life, that he may please him who has enlisted him as a soldier. (2 Timothy 2:3,4)

There is an unseen battle going on around us every day of our lives. If we could see our enemy, we could fight with material weapons. Our battle, however, is in the spiritual realm, and that requires us to use different tactics. Paul said:

> For though we walk in the flesh, we do not war according to the flesh. For the weapons of our warfare are not carnal but mighty in God for pulling down strongholds, casting down arguments and every high thing that exalts itself against the

knowledge of God, bringing every thought into captivity to the obedience of Christ. (2 Corinthians 10:3-5)

The battle for the Christian is won by recognizing the strategy of the enemy. Recognition is the first step to victory. We discussed the concept of attacking the problem, and not each other, earlier in this chapter. Instead of praying about the conflict, we find ourselves fighting against *flesh and blood*. Paul said:

> Finally, my brethren, be strong in the Lord and in the power of His might. Put on the whole armor of God, that you may be able to stand against the wiles of the devil. For we do not wrestle against flesh and blood, but against principalities, against powers, against the rulers of the darkness of this age, against spiritual hosts of wickedness in the heavenly places. Therefore take up the whole armor of God, that you may be able to withstand in the evil day, and having done all, to stand. Stand therefore, having girded your waist with truth, having put on the breastplate of righteousness, and having shod your feet with the preparation of the gospel of peace; above all, taking the shield of faith with which you will be able to quench all the fiery darts of the wicked one. And take the helmet of salvation, and the sword of the Spirit, which is the word of God. (Ephesians 6:10-17)

As Christians, we need to understand the importance of getting spiritually dressed each day for battle. How many soldiers do we know who would go to war without any armament? If they did, they would be sitting ducks just waiting to be destroyed. In the same light, many couples I have talked to do not put on the armor of God, and some have even acknowledged that they had never even heard of it. That is one of the tactics of the devil! If he can make us believe that there is no battle, we have already been conquered.

Rynner and I put on our armor in the morning before we start our day. I will begin our prayer time by praying for our specific needs, and then we get spiritually dressed. We know that we will be attacked, and we want to know that we have done all we can to stand.

We pray that God will put on our *breastplate of righteousness*, and that we will be cleansed from all of our sin. When we put on our *helmet of salvation*, we pray that the Lord will protect our minds, and that our thoughts will glorify Him throughout the day. We ask Him to put the gospel of peace on our feet. With this, we pray for a peaceful day, and that we will have an opportunity to share the Lord with anyone who might come into our path. We pray for *our waist to be girded with truth* so that we will be truthful and honest in all of our communication. Then we ask the Lord to put *the shield of faith* and *the sword of the Spirit* (which is the Word of God) in our hands. The shield so that we will have faith for all God wants to do in our lives, and the sword of the Spirit that we will be able to memorize the Scriptures so that we can encourage ourselves as well as others in times of difficulty.

The Word of God is our only offensive piece of armor, and we need to use it! When Jesus was led into the wilderness to be tempted by the devil, the Lord quoted the Word three times to him. Afterwards the Bible says, "Then the devil left Him, and behold, angels came and ministered to Him" (Matthew 4:11). We need to memorize the Word of God to counteract the lies of the enemy as well. James says:

> Therefore submit to God. Resist the devil and he will flee from you. Draw near to God and He will draw near to you. (James 4:7,8)

That is exactly what Jesus did: He resisted the devil with the Word of God, and the enemy fled from Him. We need to do the same, and we can begin by applying the armor of God each day. Once we have memorized the pieces of armor, we can incorporate our own needs into our prayer with our fiancée or spouse. Putting on the armor of God is a trebled blessing: It insures us prayer time together, it allows us to hear the needs of our loved one, and it protects us from the onslaught of the enemy during the day.

Jesus also acknowledged the power of the enemy in the life of the believer. When the disciples were with Him in the Garden of Gethsemane, before His crucifixion, they were very sleepy. Jesus said:

> What, could you not watch with Me one hour? Watch and
> pray, lest you enter into temptation. The spirit indeed is
> willing, but the flesh is weak. (Matthew 26:40,41)

We can experience the same types of temptation in our marriages. We may have a desire to read the Bible with our spouse in the evening. Now, we know the enemy does not want us to engage in any spiritual activity as a couple, and he will try to prevent us from doing so. There are all kinds of methods he uses, and we need to be aware of them. The Bible says, "We are not ignorant of his devices" (2 Corinthians 2:11). We may plan to go to a Bible study during the week, and after dinner we may all of a sudden have a feeling of exhaustion and decide to stay home. We might make plans to attend a weekend retreat for married couples, and the night before we get into an argument about something insignificant that keeps us from attending. We were recently asked to speak at a retreat for couples on the Central Coast of California. The pastor was concerned about one of the couples that seemed to be excited about the weekend beforehand, but had never arrived. He was informed the next day that the couple had gotten into a fight on the way to the retreat. They had even made it into the parking lot, and they had turned around and gone home. Another example is found in some of the prayer requests we receive in our premarital class that ask us to pray because something always happens to try to prevent them from attending. Even before we get married, we need to realize the enemy is trying to undermine the work of the Spirit in our lives. We must remember the promise of God that will encourage us during these times of attack:

> No weapon formed against you shall prosper, and every tongue
> which rises against you in judgement you shall condemn. This
> is the heritage of the servants of the LORD. (Isaiah 54:17)

This promise does not negate our responsibilities as Christians. We are instructed to put on the whole armor of God. As we are obedient to the Scriptures, and as we resist the devil, we will experience the victory when the conflicts arise.

Review Questions

Resolving Conflict

1. What seems to cause conflict in your relationship? (See James 4:1-3.)

    _____

    _____

    _____

    _____

    _____

2. What kind of answer turns away anger? (See Proverbs 15:1.)

    _____

    _____

    _____

    _____

    _____

3. When a conflict arises, how do you handle it? Do you attack the problem, or the person that you feel is the source of the conflict? Do you tend to run from the situation? What are some Scriptural remedies?

    _____

    _____

    _____

    _____

    _____

4. What does it mean to reconcile?

_____

_____

_____

_____

_____

5. Based on Ephesians 4:26,27, when should conflict be resolved?

_____

_____

_____

_____

_____

6. Why is it important to settle disputes as soon as possible?

_____

_____

_____

_____

_____

7. What are the benefits of making up quickly after a disagreement?

_____

_____

_____

_____

_____

8. Hebrews 3:13 says, "Exhort one another daily." List some practical ways you can exhort your fiancée or spouse.

a) _____

b) _____

c) _____

d) _____

e) _____

9. How is a person to speak the truth? (See Ephesians 4:15.) Give an example of how this can be accomplished.

_____

_____

_____

_____

_____

10. Read Ephesians 6:10-18. List the pieces of armor and their significance.

a) _____

_____

_____

b) _____

_____

_____

c) _____

_____

_____

d) _____

_____

_____

e) _____

_____

_____

f) _____

_____

_____

Notes

_____

_____

_____

_____

_____

_____

_____

_____

_____

_____

_____

_____

_____

_____

_____

_____

_____

_____

_____

_____

_____

_____

_____

_____

_____

Notes

_____
_____
_____
_____
_____
_____
_____
_____
_____
_____
_____
_____
_____
_____
_____
_____
_____
_____
_____
_____
_____

CHAPTER 6

The Need for Romance

Almost everyone has a need for romance in their life. This is illustrated by the fact that one of the many publishers in America sold over two hundred million romance novels in one year. I think one reason for the success in sales is that people want to experience love in their own lives, or vicariously through someone else. If it is a video, a book, or the romance in the life of a friend, we always want the ending to be "and they lived happily ever after."

Nearly every marriage begins with a romantic attraction as well. In other words, there was an attribute in your fiancée or spouse that initially drew you to them. It does not always have to involve the outward appearance, however. It could have been their love for the Lord, or their sense of humor. Some characteristic about that individual made you say, "I think there is something special about that person, and I would like to get to know them better."

What is the definition of romance? The dictionary describes it as "a long medieval narrative in prose or verse; the telling of the adventures of chivalric heroes; or stories, novels or films dealing with a love affair." We all obviously have a different idea of the definition of romance from our own experience. We are familiar with the Disney movies such as *Sleeping Beauty, Snow White*, or *Cinderella* when Prince Charming arrives on the scene, and rescues the maiden in distress. The girl sings, "Someday my prince will come." Perhaps your prince has arrived.

Romance in the Bible

Did you know that there are some great examples of romance and love stories in the Bible? One in particular is found in the Book of Song of Solomon. It is exciting to see the love that God has placed in the hearts of The Shulamite and The Beloved for one another. The Beloved says:

> You have ravished my heart, my sister, my spouse; you have ravished my heart with one look of your eyes, with one link of your necklace. How fair is your love, my sister, my spouse! How much better than wine is your love, and the scent of your perfumes than all spices! (Song of Solomon 4:9,10)

The poetry in Song of Solomon is romantic as well as descriptive. When The Beloved says, "You have ravished my heart," the word ravished means "to make the heart beat faster," or in other words, "When I see you, my heart skips a beat." The Shulamite describes this attraction by extolling the physical virtues of The Beloved to her girlfriends. She says:

> My beloved is white and ruddy, chief among ten thousand. His head is like the finest gold; his locks are wavy, and black as a raven. His eyes are like doves by the rivers of waters, washed with milk, and fitly set. His cheeks are like a bed of spices, like banks of scented herbs. His lips are lilies, dripping liquid myrrh. His hands are rods of gold set with beryl. His body is carved ivory inlaid with sapphires. His legs are pillars of marble set on bases of fine gold. His countenance is like Lebanon, excellent as the cedars. His mouth is most sweet, yes, he is altogether lovely. This is my beloved, and this is my friend, O daughters of Jerusalem! (Song of Solomon 5:10-16)

Become Friends First

We know our marital relationships usually begin strong in the realm of the physical, but we want to have them continue to thrive in this dimension, by the grace of God. How can we cultivate romance after we have taken our vows, in the midst of our busy schedules, our careers, children, and the responsibilities of life that continually pull at us? One way this couple has cultivated the love in their relationship is through friendship. The Shulamite says:

This is my beloved, and this is my friend. (Song of Solomon 5:16)

We see here that their romantic attraction is not only limited to the physical. Yes, this man is attractive. He is strong, he has beautiful wavy hair; he is a handsome guy just as she is a beautiful woman. One of the strong points of their relationship is that they were friends. Friendship is the key that will help maintain the romance in our marriage. We know that the Bible says, "A friend loves at all times" (Proverbs 17:17). But to continue the friendship and build romance in our marriage, we need to be friendly and loving to one another. Would you classify yourself as a friendly person? We know that being friendly is an act of our will. There will be times when we do not feel like being kind or loving to our fiancée or spouse, however we are called to love others as Jesus loves us. John the Beloved said:

My little children, let us not love in word or in tongue, but in deed and in truth. (1 John 3:18)

We should want to exemplify the kindness of Christ at all times. We also know that we can only exhibit these characteristics when we allow the Holy Spirit to empower us. (See John 15:4,5.) As a friend to our fiancée or spouse, we need to show love in action. We are not going to wait for them to act friendly toward us. If there has been a misunderstanding between us, we have to try to resolve the conflict. I was talking to a gentleman the other day who was having problems with his wife. He explained to her that he had several insecurities regarding relationships, and he asked her if she would help him work with his shortcomings. Her response was, "Don't expect me to help you with your problems." It was evident that she did not want to resolve the conflict by her lack of love and concern. She was not acting like a wife to her husband, let alone like *a friend*! We know that conflict destroys romance; it destroys the love God intended us to have with one another. Romance is built upon active daily communication and kindness.

Friendship is developed through communication. If you are a woman, you probably have friends that you go with to lunch, or talk to on the phone regularly.

Guys, you probably have friends at the office, or someone you have known from college with whom you keep in touch. You are interested in what he shares with you. You listen to him when he is contemplating a job change, or if he wants your opinion on a girl he is dating. Friendship in marriage is the same. We need to show an interest in our fiancée or spouse by spending time together on a daily basis.

When Rynner and I met, we became friends right away. We spent hours and hours talking over coffee after church at local restaurants. We could not learn enough about each other! We can both say that there were no surprises regarding one another after we got married. We were best friends, and we still are because of the time we spend together. We make it a point to protect our time together, and we encourage others to do the same.

There was a strong attraction between these two individuals in the Song of Solomon. It began in the physical, but their love for one another grew to a deeper level. A bond developed and they confessed that their love had become as strong as death; even fire could not quench it! The Shulamite said to The Beloved:

> Set me as a seal upon your heart, as a seal upon your arm; for love is as strong as death, jealousy as cruel as the grave; its flames are flames of fire, a most vehement flame. Many waters cannot quench love, nor can the floods drown it. If a man would give for love all the wealth of his house, it would be utterly despised. (Song of Solomon 8:6,7)

How can we continue to build romance in our relationship as the years pass? We mentioned the importance of spending time together, and one basic way to do this is by making an effort to eat one or two meals together every day. (I know, if someone were to read that statement one hundred years ago, it would sound ridiculous!) It seems that everyone is always on the go in our society today. The husband leaves early in the morning for a meeting while the wife eats an apple in the car while driving the children to school. There can be a similar scenario at dinnertime: One of the children has a sports event, and the husband ends up having to work late. The only thing that seems to connect all of us is the cellular phone, or the answering machine. There are ways, however, to build romance in a marriage even with our hectic way of life. We should plan to eat together even if it means adjusting our schedules and eating later.

We need to stay current with one another as we relate the blessings and the struggles of our day. Rynner and I used to share just the highlights at meals when we were newlyweds. She wanted to hear the details of my day as well as tell me what she experienced. (Remember those 25,000 words?) I have now grown accustomed to a lengthy dinnertime because we have so much to communicate with each other, and I have found that I really enjoy it. I feel like I have walked with her through the day and she with me. We do not want to let months and years go by where we become "married singles." This is when we are married, but we do everything separately. Oh, we may get twice as much accomplished, but we will quench the romance in our relationship.

The Potter and the Clay

A friend will not try to control their fiancée or spouse. On the contrary, they allow God to work in His timing in the life of the other person. We may see areas in our loved ones that we do not like, and sometimes we want to be the instrument to initiate change. We want to mold and shape them into our image, and how we think they should be. But changing people is not our responsibility. Isaiah said, "But now, O LORD, You are our Father; we are the clay, and You our potter; and all we are the work of Your hand" (Isaiah 64:8). God, the Master Potter does the changing, and all we are called to do is pray for our fiancée or spouse. A woman we know tried to change her husband for several years and nothing she suggested ever worked. As she was praying one day, the Lord gave her a picture in her mind of a potter working on two clay pots on two separate wheels. Both the wheels were spinning and the potter was changing aspects of each pot at different times. At one point, a *clay hand* came out of one of the pots, and attempted to mold and shape the other clay pot. The clay hand got stuck all over the second pot, and both of the pots were marred. The potter had to start over to remake each pot. The Lord showed this woman that she was one of these clay pots, and that her husband was the other. The clay hand was her hand coming out of her pot as she tried to change her husband into the man she wanted him to be. She was trying to be the Holy Spirit in his life, and God showed her that she was to stop trying to change her husband with her words and helpful suggestions. She was to pray, and let the Lord do the work. We do not know what is best for our lives, or the life of our spouse, but God does. He is the Master Potter who is molding each of us, and we need to leave the changing of our spouse in the hands of God.

Be Spontaneous

Romance is also built by being unpredictable and spontaneous. Men, do we need to take "Being Creative in our Relationship 101" again? There are some people who are just naturally creative. One man we knew proposed to his fiancée by chartering a private plane, and flying her to a desolate airstrip in the desert. They landed, and at the end of the runway there was a beautiful table set with fine linen, china, and a catered dinner. He pulled out a little black box with the ring, and asked her to marry him. Now that is original! We all do not have the gift of creativity perhaps, but we can pray that God will keep the romance in our relationship alive and to help us in this area. Here is a list of a few simple things we can do to build our romance:

- Send her flowers for no reason.

- Put a note on the windshield of his/her car.

- Mail a romantic card to him/her.

- Slip a note in his jacket pocket to find at a later date.

- Leave an e-mail on his/her computer.

- Make his favorite cookies, and leave them on his desk at work with a love note.

- Take a walk where it is quiet and scenic in the evening.

We can plan special times to be together. Sometimes we think we have to plan lavishly in order to have our loved one really remember the event, but that is not true. A couple we know meets every Monday for lunch at a park, and they pray for their own needs, as well as the needs of others. They love it! It is a time that they can count on to be with one another while including a spiritual activity. Even if we do not have time to meet for lunch, a phone call can encourage our spouse. We can tell them we love them, and we can pray for them.

Husbands, we do not want to take our wives for granted. After we have been married a while, we can ask our wife out on a date. We can invite them to a special restaurant by sending a card in the mail, or on their computer via e-mail. We could also take them away to a Bed and Breakfast for the weekend, and not let them know beforehand where we are going. We need to pray about it, and be creative. A friend of mine surprised his wife by taking her to Cancún, Mexico for a week. Unbeknownst to her, he called her place of work and arranged the vacation time with her boss. A couple of days before they left he gave her instructions of what to pack, and not to worry about anything else. She was amazed at the thoughtfulness of her husband! This is one of the ways we can keep our love alive although our ideas do not have to be as expensive. A lot of times, these extravagant plans can put financial pressure on us. We can do something as simple as make our wife a cup of coffee on a Saturday morning, sit down at the table, and ask them how their week has been. Believe me, it will really bless them! Pray with them regarding their needs. They will be blown away, and they will appreciate us more than we know!

In the Song of Solomon, The Beloved and The Shulamite took a romantic walk together to observe the creation of God. It says:

> My beloved spoke, and said to me: "Rise up, my love, my fair one, and come away. For lo, the winter is past, the rain is over and gone. The flowers appear on the earth; the time of singing has come, and the voice of the turtledove is heard in our land. The fig tree puts forth her green figs, and the vines with the tender grapes give a good smell. Rise up, my love, my fair one, and come away!" (Song of Solomon 2:10-13)

God created nature for our enjoyment, and that is why I feel it is important for us as couples to get outdoors whenever we can. Rynner and I love to take walks together down by the beach. It is so relaxing to look at the boats on the water, and to smell the salt in the air. Our relationship is nurtured as we walk hand in hand. There are no phones or doorbells to answer, and we can converse with one another freely. We can also bring our prayer requests before the Lord as we walk because there are no distractions. We will go back and forth with our requests; I will pray for an area in our lives, and then she will follow with a request, and so forth. It is one of our favorite activities to do as a couple.

Keeping Our Romance Alive

In the Song of Solomon we see how important it is for us to keep ourselves physically attractive for our fiancée or spouse. The Beloved said to The Shulamite:

> How beautiful are your feet in sandals, O prince's daughter! [*Do you see how he noticed her new shoes, and commented on them?*] Your neck is like an ivory tower, your eyes like the pools in Heshbon by the gate of Bath Rabbim. Your nose is like the tower of Lebanon which looks toward Damascus. Your head crowns you like Mount Carmel, and the hair of your head is like purple; the king is held captive by its tresses. How fair and how pleasant you are, O love, with your delights! (Song of Solomon 7:1,4-6)

The Bible says, "Even though our outward man is perishing, yet the inward man is being renewed day by day" (2 Corinthians 4:16). We need to concentrate more on the spiritual than the physical, however, we do not want to neglect taking care of the temple that God has given us. (See 1 Corinthians 6:19,20.) It is so easy to take the time to look nice when we are dating or engaged, but the challenge arises to continue to keep ourselves attractive after we have been married for a while. What did you do to prepare for your first date? I am sure you wanted to look your best. Men, you showered and shaved, you brushed your teeth, and you probably even got a haircut. Women, you put on perfume, and took time to look your best. Solomon said, "[The virtuous woman] girds herself with strength, and strengthens her arms" (Proverbs 31:17). If it means walking with a friend in the morning, or putting on a little make-up , continue taking care of yourself, and it will be a blessing to your spouse.

There are other ways to keep our romance alive. We can do this through the words we speak, and in our expression of physical love. Men, when was the last time you told your fiancée or your spouse that you loved her, that she is beautiful, or that you liked her new sweater just like The Beloved commented on the shoes of The Shulamite? We need to take notice of these things. (Now women, it is important that you take note of this because if he does not speak encouraging words before you get married, chances are he will not after you take your vows. Remember we cannot change each other; that is up to the Lord.) Likewise, women, when was the last time you thanked your fiancé or your spouse for changing your oil, for taking you to dinner, or for his diligence to save for your future? We need to show our appreciation and thanks to each other, and as we do we can change the direction of our relationship by the words we use. Encouraging one another helps to build romance; tearing each other down destroys it.

Physical Love

We also can express our physical love by doing something as simple as holding hands when we go into church, when we go into a supermarket, or a mall. After we get married, we can give each other a kiss or a hug when we pass one another in the hallway of our home. (It is surprising to know the number of couples who do not do these kinds of things!) If your wife is rinsing the dishes after dinner, you can give her a little back rub, or offer to put the dishes in the dishwasher for her. You could even tell her to sit down and relax while *you* do the dishes! These are all expressions of love that we want to maintain throughout our relationship.

The ultimate way we show our physical love for one another is through sexual intimacy. This is an act that God has reserved for husbands and wives *only,* and it is a beautiful thing. It allows us to demonstrate our love for one another, and it is a blessing! He designed it for our pleasure, and it is to be enjoyed throughout marriage.

The Bible says:

> Now concerning the things of which you wrote to me: It is good for a man not to touch a woman. Nevertheless, because of sexual immorality, let each man have his own wife, and let each woman have her own husband. Let the husband render to his wife the affection due her, and likewise also the wife to her husband. The wife does not have authority over her own body, but the husband does. And likewise the husband does not have authority over his own body, but the wife does. Do not deprive one another except with consent for a time, that you may give yourselves to fasting and prayer; and come together again so that Satan does not tempt you because of your lack of self-control. But I say this as a concession, not as a commandment. (1 Corinthians 7:1-6)

As Christians, we want to reserve this sacred union for our wedding night. Unfortunately, we are bombarded with stimuli related to sex almost every day of our lives. We may be tempted to listen to the lies of Satan and say, "Why should we wait until we get married? We are engaged now, and we are committed to one another." We want to obey the Word of God, and keep the act of making love special and holy to the Lord. Fornication is addressed in several places in the Word of God. The Apostle Paul warned the churches in Galatia and Corinth against this sin. He said:

> I say then: Walk in the Spirit, and you shall not fulfill the lust of the flesh. For the flesh lusts against the Spirit, and the Spirit against the flesh; and these are contrary to one another, so that you do not do the things that you wish. But if you are led by the Spirit, you are not under the law. Now the works of the flesh are evident, which are: adultery, fornication, uncleanness, licentiousness, idolatry, sorcery, hatred, contentions, jealousies, outbursts of wrath, selfish ambitions, dissensions, heresies, envy, murders, drunkenness, revelries, and the like; of which I tell you beforehand, just as I also told you in time past, that those who practice such things will not inherit the kingdom of God. (Galatians 5:16-21)

Do you not know that the unrighteous will not inherit the kingdom of God? Do not be deceived. Neither fornicators, nor idolaters, nor adulterers, nor homosexuals, nor sodomites, nor thieves, nor covetous, nor drunkards, nor revilers, nor extortioners will inherit the kingdom of God. And such were some of you. But you were washed, but you were sanctified, but you were justified in the name of the Lord Jesus and by the Spirit of our God. (1 Corinthians 6:9-11)

Fornication is sex before marriage, and fornicators will not inherit the kingdom of God. These are heavy Scriptures. If we are dating, or engaged to a person who thinks that we can have sex before marriage, and still be in the center of the will of God, we are deceived. We need to reevaluate our relationship with them! We have talked to many couples who have struggled in this area, some willfully, and some out of ignorance. Some have argued that they have had to move in together for financial reasons, but they are sleeping in separate rooms. This is contrary to the Word of God which says, "Abstain from *all appearance* of evil" (1 Thessalonians 5:22 KJV)[Emphasis mine]. The Lord says this because He knows how great the temptation would be in such a situation, not to mention the poor witness it is to others. The Bible asks, "Can a man take fire to his bosom, and his clothes not be burned" (Proverbs 6:27)? Sin will separate us from God and from one another. We want the Lord to be the center of our relationship, and we can do this by waiting until we get married to enjoy the gift of physical love that He has given us.

If we have had difficulties in this area, we definitely need to take it to the Lord in prayer. He can help us to get the victory, and abstain until we are married. We need to agree on a few guidelines. Here are some suggestions:

- We need to spend as much time as we can with groups of people so that we will be accountable for our behavior.

- We need to set a reasonable curfew when we get together for a date.

- We will not kiss each other in the car when we are alone.

- We will not discuss our future physical relationship.

- We will not visit one another at our homes if no one else is there.

You may read these guidelines and say, "I am an adult, and I am able to handle myself." Be careful, because the Bible says, "Pride goes before destruction, and a haughty spirit before a fall" (Proverbs 16:18). The enemy is subtle, and he will try to use your self-acclaimed maturity against you. If we avoid these types of situations in the first place, it will keep us from having to make decisions in the heat of passion when we are weak and vulnerable later.

The Differences Between Men and Women

We know men and women have different needs, and this is demonstrated by some statistics taken by Willard F. Harley in his book, *His Needs, Her Needs.*[6] The results were very interesting:

The Five Basic Needs of a Man	The Five Basic Needs of a Woman

1. Sexual fulfillment

2. Recreational companionship

3. An attractive spouse

4. Domestic support

5. Admiration

1. Affection

2. Conversation

3. Honesty and openness

4. Financial support

5. Family commitment

Notice the difference between what men desire in a relationship contrasted with those of a woman. Sexual fulfillment is not even on her list! Women need to be cared for and loved, and that does not necessarily mean going into the bedroom. I think of times I have counseled married couples who have had a disagreement, and the husband wanted to reconcile by making love. That was probably the last thing the woman wanted to do! She was thinking, "He does not care about my heart, or what I am feeling. He simply wants to fulfill his own physical needs." Men want sex, and women want tenderness and affection, and there is a difference between the two. Men, we need to be sensitive to our wives in this area.

We know from the Scriptures that we are not to withhold ourselves from our spouse physically. The Bible says:

> Do not deprive one another except with consent for a time,
> that you may give yourselves to fasting and prayer; and come
> together again so that Satan does not tempt you because of
> your lack of self-control. (1 Corinthians 7:5)

We are not to use sex as a bartering tool, or in manipulation of any kind. The Word of God says that our body belongs to our spouse, and we are to minister to them physically if they have that need.

We have looked at many ways to keep romance alive in our marriage. We can see from the Song of Solomon that romance in marriage goes beyond physical expression. More importantly, it is based on a husband and a wife being friends: A friendship where we look to fulfill the needs of each other.

Review Questions

Romance

1. What is your definition of romance?

    _____

    _____

    _____

    _____

    _____

2. What first attracted you to your fiancée or spouse?

    _____

    _____

    _____

    _____

3. The Bible says, "A friend loves at all times" (Proverbs 17:17). Would you describe yourself as a friendly person? If so, how do you show it?

    _____

    _____

    _____

    _____

4. What we say to each other will either encourage or discourage the romance in our relationship. Is there anything you have been saying that could be hindering your romance? (See Ephesians 4:32.)

_____

_____

_____

_____

_____

5. Romance is built by being unpredictable and spontaneous. List a few ideas of ways you can be spontaneous with your fiancée or spouse.

    a) _____

    b) _____

    c) _____

    d) _____

    e) _____

6. What do you think is your greatest need in marriage?

_____

_____

_____

_____

_____

7. Considering 1 John 3:18, list some tangible ways you can express your love?

    a) _____

    b) _____

    c) _____

    d) _____

8. List some of the things that could hinder romance in marriage?

_____

_____

_____

_____

_____

9. Read Isaiah 64:8. We need to remember that God is going to change your fiancée or spouse in His timing. In light of this, are there any weaknesses they have that you need to surrender to the Lord?

_____

_____

_____

_____

_____

10. Knowing what the Scriptures say regarding sex before marriage, what steps are you taking to abstain, and to keep yourselves pure before the Lord?

_____

_____

_____

_____

_____

11. What does it mean to "abstain from all appearance of evil" (1 Thessalonians 5:22 KJV)?

_____

_____

_____

_____

Notes

Notes

Notes

_____
_____
_____
_____
_____
_____
_____
_____
_____
_____
_____
_____
_____
_____
_____
_____
_____
_____
_____
_____
_____
_____

CHAPTER 7

For Richer, or For Poorer

Contentment

In a few months or so, you will be taking your vows of marriage at the altar and saying, "For better, or for worse; for richer, or for poorer; in sickness, and in health; until death do us part." Even with this commitment, one out of every two marriages ends in divorce in America, whether they are Christian or not. The statistics for divorce change dramatically for those couples that pray together on a regular basis. The reasons for divorce vary, but in every survey we have read, financial difficulty is at the top of the list. Because of this, we need to go into marriage in prayer about our financial situation!

In the preceding chapter we listed the five basic needs of husbands and wives. The need for financial support was number four on the list for the woman. It is an important aspect, and we should become acquainted with the saving, and the spending habits of our fiancée before our wedding day.

The Bible covers nearly every aspect of life, and we want to look at our finances from a Scriptural point of view. The Apostle Paul said:

> But godliness with contentment is great gain. For we brought nothing into this world, and it is certain we can carry nothing out. And having food and clothing, with these we shall be content. But those who desire to be rich fall into temptation and a snare, and into many foolish and harmful lusts which drown men in destruction and perdition. For the love of money is a root of all kinds of evil, for which some have strayed from the faith in their greediness, and pierced themselves through with many sorrows. But you, O man of God, flee these things and pursue righteousness, godliness, faith, love, patience, gentleness. Fight the good fight of faith, lay hold on eternal life, to which you were also called and have confessed the good confession in the presence of many witnesses. (1 Timothy 6:6-12)

The question we want to ask ourselves is, "Are we content where God has put us financially?" One of the best definitions I have found regarding contentment is:

Contentment is not having all you want, but wanting only what you have.

The subject of contentment can be a challenge because the society in which we live bombards us daily with the advertisements on television, in newspapers, and in magazines of what we need to make our lives more fulfilling. We may have dreams of climbing the corporate ladder, taking European vacations, or buying that long-awaited sports utility vehicle. The challenge of Paul is that we would be satisfied with what God has provided for us today.

The Greek word for contentment in this passage of the Bible means self-sufficiency. It is having what we need, and not striving for more. If we seek after riches, we will fall into temptation. The Apostle Paul said:

> Not that I speak in regard to need, for I have learned in whatever state I am, to be content: I know how to be abased, and I know how to abound. Everywhere and in all things I have learned both to be full and to be hungry, both to abound and to suffer need. I can do all things through Christ who strengthens me. (Philippians 4:11-13)

True fulfillment in life comes only from having a relationship with the Lord Jesus Christ, and knowing that He will provide for all of our needs.

Now I am not decrying those who have wealth, nor am I saying that having financial goals in life is wrong. We need, however, to keep our finances in their proper perspective. Jesus said, "But seek first the kingdom of God and His righteousness, and all these things shall be added to you" (Matthew 6:33). He also said, "Take heed and beware of covetousness, for one's life does not consist in the abundance of the things he possesses" (Luke 12:15). Our society teaches us that if we possess certain material items, we are successful. The world says, "Borrow from the future in order to live today." We want to appear successful by having a large home, nice cars, and all of the "toys" for our weekend excursions. Some couples have even had to declare bankruptcy because they could not curtail their spending. If we engage in this type of behavior it could put pressure on our relationship, and cause conflict. Only a right relationship with Jesus Christ will give us the contentment we need to abstain from the worldly lusts around us. (See 1 Peter 2:11,12.)

Beware of Prosperity Teachers

There is a heretical teaching in the body of Christ that is called *The Word of Faith Movement*. The leaders in this movement claim that God wants every believer to be wealthy. If you are not, you are lacking in faith, and you are not in the will of God. Essentially they say, "Name what you want, and then claim it!" As believers, we do not *claim* anything that is not contained in the Word of God. God knows what is best for us, and He will give us what we need. The Apostle Peter said:

> [God in] His divine power has given to us all things that pertain to life and godliness, through the knowledge of Him who called us by glory and virtue, by which have been given to us exceedingly great and precious promises, that through these you may be partakers of the divine nature, having escaped the corruption that is in the world through lust. (2 Peter 1:3,4)

This teaching is contrary to Scripture because Jesus said, "Blessed are you poor, for yours is the kingdom of God" (Luke 6:20). He also said, "For you have the poor with you always" (Mark 14:7). These verses indicate that there will always be poor Christians living on the earth. Have you ever gone down to Mexico, or to a third world country to minister to the believers? When we lived in England we met many Christians who had very little with which to live. They were not lacking in faith; they loved the Lord with all their hearts! God has ordained a social standing for each of His children, and He wants to teach us lessons wherever we are in life. What the Faith Movement teaches is a lie from the enemy, and it has caused a lot of damage in Christian homes.

133

Paul said, "For the love of money is a root of all kinds of evil, for which some have strayed from the faith in their greediness, and pierced themselves through with many sorrows" (1 Timothy 6:10). Money is a necessary commodity in life, and we cannot survive without it. When it is not in its proper perspective, however, it can begin to rule us. What are your financial goals as a couple? Are you content with what you have? These are important questions to ask because we may find that our fiancée has goals in the next ten years to work long hours in order to own the newest Mercedes, and to buy a home in the best part of town. Maybe you are content with the simple things in life. You may want to have a couple of children, and spend a lot of family time together. Perhaps you have even thought of becoming a missionary! All of these issues regarding finances need to be discussed thoroughly because they can bring stress later on in your marriage.

We know that it is not a sin to be wealthy. There are people mentioned in the Bible who ministered to Jesus because they had excess, and wanted to provide for Him and His disciples. We know several couples who are financially secure, and they use their income to bless the body of Christ as well. These people love the Lord, and are a wonderful witness. Conversely, there are multimillionaires like Cornelius Vanderbilt who when he was asked, "When is enough [money] enough?" He answered, "Just one dollar more." With all of his riches, he was not content! Now, we may not be as financially secure as we would like to be, but our attitude could be the same. We could be covetous, and have a continual longing for more.

Take Inventory

The Bible says, "For if we would judge ourselves, we would not be judged" (1 Corinthians 11:31). We need to take the time and examine our hearts in the light of the Word of God. Are we covetous? Are we looking for that new car or a new wardrobe to fulfill us? Can we exercise self-control in our spending, or do we pull out the plastic if we cannot afford an item? The Lord can help us control our spending if we will just give Him a chance!

There are steps we can take to keep from becoming discontent with our financial circumstances. One step is to take inventory of what is influencing us on a day to day basis. What magazines are we reading? What television shows are we watching? What kind of friends do we have? How much time do we spend in the Word of God? Are we involved in a weekly Bible study? These are very relevant questions we can ask ourselves. If we are watching game shows on television, and buying lottery tickets every day without offsetting that mentality with what the Bible teaches, we are going to find ourselves in trouble in the future. The perspective God wants us to have will fade while the mercenary within us takes over, and this mindset can destroy our marriage.

The Apostle Paul said, "But you, O man of God, flee these things and pursue righteousness, godliness, faith, love, patience, gentleness" (1 Timothy 6:11). We are to "seek first the kingdom of God and His righteousness, and all these things shall be added to [us]" (Matthew 6:33). God promises to provide for all of our needs as long as we put Him first in our lives.

The Parable of the Rich Fool

There is a portion of Scripture that speaks about this subject in the Book of Luke. Jesus said, "Take heed and beware of covetousness, for one's life does not consist in the abundance of the things he possesses" (Luke 12:15). Then He shared a parable with them and said:

> The ground of a certain rich man yielded plentifully. And he thought within himself, saying, "What shall I do, since I have no room to store my crops?" So he said, "I will do this: I will pull down my barns and build greater, and there I will store all my crops and my goods. And I will say to my soul, 'Soul, you have many goods laid up for many years; take your ease; eat, drink, and be merry.'" But God said to him, "You fool! This night your soul will be required of you; then whose will those things be which you have provided?" So is he who lays up

treasure for himself, and is not rich toward God. (Luke 12:16-21)

This man had his priorities in the wrong place, and we do not want to be deceived in the same way. We were not placed on earth to build our little empire. We were created for fellowship with God, and to bring others to the saving knowledge of Jesus Christ. We must guard our hearts against the snare in which the world wants to trap us, because "where [our] treasure is, there [our] heart will be also" (Luke 12:34).

Where are our hearts? Where is our treasure? What have we been pursuing? What is the all consuming passion that gets us out of bed each morning? This rich man was laying up his treasure on earth. We have a friend who did the same thing when he was newly married. He wanted to have fun, and in order to do that he had to borrow because he wanted to satisfy his fleshly desires. He told his wife that he just had to have a board for windsurfing. She kept a good record of the finances, and she said, "Honey, we just had a baby, and we cannot afford it!" He did not listen to her warnings. He went out and charged one on their credit card. Would you believe that the day after he purchased it, the board was stolen? He had to make payments on a $500 windsurfing board that he could not use! He certainly learned the lesson of overspending the hard way.

I also read recently that Elton John spends $400,000 a week on credit cards, and he is $40 million dollars in debt. He has six homes, and he has a florist on retainer who puts fresh flowers in every room of every home, whether he is staying there, or not. Talk about extravagance! I think we can all see with all of the costumes, the glasses, the servants, and the trips how it all adds up. His creditors are now attaching his royalties and future projects in order to pay his debt. How sad it is that with all of the millions and millions of dollars he has made, he cannot live within his means. He has amassed so much, and yet he still is not satisfied.

Live a Simple Life

We are not going to take anything with us when we die. As we all have heard, "There are no U-hauls behind a hearse." It is so important that we live a simple life. We need to learn to be content with what we have, and if there is something we need or desire, we should pray about it. The Bible says, "Your Father knows the things you have need of before you ask Him" (Matthew 6:8). He will direct us as to the timing of the purchase, or He may even provide a miracle!

The Lord showed us many miracles when we were newly married. We both were working at the time, but I was hoping to change my field of work which was landscape architecture. We prayed one night about the desires I felt God had put in my heart. The next day I was laid off from my job! When I arrived home that night, I told Rynner what had transpired. I know this sounds crazy, but she grabbed my hands, and began jumping around the room. She was so excited because of the prayer we had prayed the night before. We both knew the Lord was working in our lives! This took place during the recession in the 1980's, and we knew there were going to be challenges ahead. I worked on my resume, and began to fill out applications for jobs in the field I desired. One day Rynner came home from work feeling very ill. She was sick for several weeks, and finally ended up quitting her job because we knew she would not be going back. We were under great financial stress, but we knew that this was a test from the Lord. Rynner began to gain strength, so she was able to get back into fellowship, and we were at church four times a week. We absorbed every Bible study, and we applied them to what we were experiencing. Every time we attended church, Pastor Chuck miraculously said something that applied to our situation, and we were hanging on his every word!

A Knock on the Door

As time passed, we began to get further and further behind in our bills. We tried to work with our creditors, and they were very kind to us because of our situation. However, every financial institution has its limitations. One evening while we were relaxing at home, a knock sounded on the door. I opened it only to find the Orange County Marshal standing before me serving me an eviction notice! We knew something like this had to happen sooner or later. We thanked him kindly, and he gave us a look like, "What planet are you two from?" We thought to ourselves, "Why should we be angry? The Bible says, "And we know that all things work together for good to those who love God, to those who are the called according to His purpose" (Romans 8:28). We knew we were not in this situation because of sin in our lives, or willful negligence on our part. We knew that verse in Jeremiah that says, "For I know the thoughts that I think toward you, says the LORD, thoughts of peace and not of evil, to give you a future and a hope" (Jeremiah 29:11). We held on to these Scriptures with a *death grip*.

One important point we need to add here is that we did not tell anyone. We knew the verse that said, "I have been young, and now am old; yet I have not seen the righteous forsaken, nor his descendants begging bread" (Psalm 37:25). We knew that if we told our parents, or people at church, they might feel the guilt of needing to give us money. If we did receive gifts under that pretense, it would not have been a miracle. God knew our needs and we wanted to solely rely upon Him. We felt if He got us into this situation, He had a reason for it, and He would certainly get us out.

God Provided

The Lord did encourage us, and showed us many miracles as the months passed. We received anonymous cashier's checks on our car window, there were groceries left on our doorstep, and cash in our mailbox! These things could have been easily stolen, but God protected it all. We were in awe at His goodness to us. We were so blessed at the love of the Christian body as well. Even though we did not tell anyone, there were evidently several people in our fellowship who were very sensitive to the Holy Spirit. The Lord can minister to us through each other as we wait on Him in prayer, and that is exactly what happened. We do not know to this day who provided for us during that time, but we know their reward is waiting for them in heaven.

The day of our eviction arrived, but we were not exactly prepared to leave. We were not being stubborn; we just thought God might want to provide another miracle. We had our time of Bible study in the morning, and then we waited on the Lord. We had to be out of our home by 1:00 p.m., and by 11:00 a.m. we thought we had better start packing some things in boxes. We were not sure what our future held, but we knew God was going before us. I rented a moving van, and without telling anyone, my wife and I moved everything in our home—appliances and all! We put everything in a storage unit in Santa Ana, and then we went back to our home to get our houseplants.

Nowhere to Go

We were not sure where we were going to sleep that night. We thought we would probably have to sleep in our car. We were good friends with a girl who lived around the corner from us who had just left on her honeymoon. She left us her key, and asked us if we would water her plants every few days while she was in Yosemite. We agreed, and when the time came for us to dispose of our plants I said to Rynner, "Let's put our plants on Diane's patio for now." As we put the last load in her backyard, the phone rang. We did not feel we should answer it because that was not one of the things she had asked us to do. However, when we realized the volume was up, and we heard Diane's voice saying, "John or Rynner, are you there?" It was then that my wife ran over to the phone, and picked up the receiver. Rynner said, "Diane, why are you calling your own home on your honeymoon? You knew no one would be here!" She said, "We felt compelled by the Lord to call home." Wow! What a miracle! Rynner felt that

God wanted her to tell them what we had experienced, and after she finished Diane said, "We are going to be gone for two weeks; stay at our place until we get back." We nearly passed out! The fingerprint of God was certainly on this situation.

We got showered, and changed into some clothes we had with us. We went to a dinner party at the home of some friends in Tustin to watch *Ben Hur*. No one there had any idea what we had gone through that day, and we did not say anything. We will never forget that evening!

The Professional Housesitters

We had a phone number where we could be reached where there was an answering machine, and I picked up our messages daily. After ten days or so of staying at the home of the honeymooners, we received a phone call. The mother-in-law of a friend was going to Mexico for two weeks, and she wanted to know if we could housesit for her because we did not have any children. We laughed to ourselves, we called her back, and told her we would love to do it. We became the professional housesitters! We went from place to place without even so much as a day in between. I believe there were only a couple of nights in the course of several months when we slept at the house of some friends. The Lord was also gracious enough to let us housesit at a home on the bay in Newport over the week of our anniversary. Talk about going in style! The husband and wife even gave us access to their large pantry and refrigerator "so the food would not spoil" while they were on their vacation. God was so good to us, and He provided all we needed.

After several months of taking care of the homes of people while they were away, an announcement was made from the pulpit at the Thursday night Bible study. Our pastor needed someone to minister to his aged aunt in her home. I nudged Rynner, and said, "I think that announcement is for us." I went up to Pastor Chuck after the study, and told him that we were available. He said that he had never thought of a couple, so he wanted to pray about it. The next day he told us that it was fine. We moved in with a few seasonal clothes and a hair dryer, and we began taking care of

Aunt Lois. We joked with each other that under these conditions, we could probably be missionaries.

We have so many stories we could share about this time in our lives, but one interesting one is Lois never liked to eat at home. Eating out gave her a reason to get dressed for the day, and it always seemed that we would run into people we knew while we were out. She enjoyed the fellowship. We went out to restaurants for breakfast, lunch, and dinner. After a few months we persuaded her to have a protein shake for breakfast, and then eat out for only two meals. She was definitely an adventure! It was fun, though, because Rynner and I have always had a heart for elderly people. When we ended our stint of taking care of her, we could have written *The Restaurant Guide to Orange County!*

While we lived with Aunt Lois, we were able to get back on our feet financially. I got a great job, and Rynner's health was improving every day. We were even able to start saving, and the future was looking bright for us once again. God truly provided for all of our needs, from the moment the Marshal came to our door until the day we were able to move into our own apartment. The words of the hymn by Fanny Crosby come to mind:

> All the way my Savior leads me; what have I to ask beside?
> Can I doubt His tender mercy, Who thro' life has been my guide?
> Heavenly peace, divinest comfort, Here by faith in Him to dwell!
> For I know whate'er befall me, Jesus doeth all things well.[7]

The Lord does do all things well, but how different the scenario could have been if we had told our friends about the plight in which we found ourselves. What if we would have asked our parents or someone in our church for a loan? What if we would have used our charge card, and stayed in a motel for all of those months? What kinds of bills would we have had to pay? By leaning on the Lord alone, we were able to watch Him meet our every need. When we give our testimony, and people ask us now if it was all worth it, we always say, "Yes." We would do it all over again because of the wonderful lessons we learned. It put spiritual meat on our bones as new believers, and it has given us faith for the tests He has put us through since then. To God be the glory, great things He hath done!

What Are We Pursuing?

The Apostle Paul said, "I have learned in whatever state I am, to be content" (Philippians 4:11). We have also had to learn to be content through all of these circumstances we have endured over the years. We have definitely learned what we can live without! Eleven years later, we had an opportunity to go to London, England to become missionaries for six months. We put everything we owned into storage again, and what did we take with us? Some warm clothes and a hair dryer!

The enemy wants to do anything he can to distract us, and get our eyes off of the Lord. We need to remind ourselves that we are pilgrims and sojourners on the earth, and we do not want to become too comfortable. (See 1 Peter 2:11). Pastor Chuck shares a quote on occasion that is very soul-searching:

There is only one life, and it will soon be passed.
Only what we do for Christ will last.

Oftentimes, we believe the lies of the enemy that the acquisition of material possessions will bring us fulfillment and satisfaction. We need to be aware of his tactics because all we see is going to perish! Peter said:

> But the day of the Lord will come as a thief in the night, in which the heavens will pass away with a great noise, and the elements will melt with fervent heat; both the earth and the works that are in it will be burned up. Therefore, since all these things will be dissolved, what manner of persons ought you to be in holy conduct and godliness, looking for and hastening the coming of the day of God, because of which the heavens will be dissolved being on fire, and the elements will melt with fervent heat? (2 Peter 3:10-12)

We need to ask ourselves some pointed questions when it comes to living in our materialistic society:

- Where is our treasure?

- Are we caught up with the cares of this life?

- Are we spending all of our time pursuing material things that are going to melt away?

- Do we both share the same financial goals?

The Scriptures promise us that God will meet all of our needs. May we pursue righteousness, learn to be content with the simple things in life, and use what we do have to further His kingdom.

Review Questions

For Richer, or for Poorer

1. What does it mean to be content?

   _____

   _____

   _____

   _____

   _____

2. Why is "godliness with contentment great gain" (1 Timothy 6:6)?

   _____

   _____

   _____

   _____

   _____

3. We know that finances can cause great conflict in marriages today. Do you both share the same financial goals? If so, what are they?

   _____

   _____

   _____

   _____

   _____

4. Jesus said, "For where your treasure is, there your heart will be also" (Luke 12:34). Make a list of the things you have been pursuing.

    a) _____

    b) _____

    c) _____

    d) _____

    e) _____

5. What does it mean to be covetous?

    _____

    _____

    _____

    _____

    _____

6. Are you aware of any financial difficulties that your fiancée or spouse is experiencing at this point in their life? (e.g. credit card debt, school loans, etc.)

    _____

    _____

    _____

    _____

    _____

7. List the principles you find in each Scripture passage:

    a) Proverbs 11:24,25

    _____

    _____

    _____

    _____

b) Proverbs 11:28

_____

_____

_____

_____

_____

c) Proverbs 12:11

_____

_____

_____

_____

_____

d) Proverbs 13:18,22

_____

_____

_____

_____

_____

e) Proverbs 15:16,17

_____

_____

_____

_____

_____

f) Proverbs 16:8

_____

_____

_____

_____

_____

g) Proverbs 20:4,13

_____

_____

_____

_____

_____

h) Proverbs 23:4,5

_____

_____

_____

_____

_____

i) Proverbs 28:6,22

_____

_____

_____

_____

_____

j) Luke 12:13-21

_____

_____

_____

_____

_____

k) Romans 13:6,7

_____

_____

_____

_____

l) Ephesians 4:28

_____

_____

_____

_____

m) Philippians 4:11-13,19

_____

_____

_____

_____

n) 2 Thessalonians 3:7-13

_____

_____

_____

_____

_____

o) 1 Timothy 6:6-12

_____

_____

_____

_____

_____

p) 1 Timothy 6:17-19

_____

_____

_____

_____

_____

q) Hebrews 13:5

_____

_____

_____

_____

_____

Notes

Notes

CHAPTER EIGHT

In-Laws

In-Laws or Out-Laws?

I think we realize when we get married, it is not going to be just the two of us. We might have to build relationships with a whole host of new people from the parents of our fiancée or spouse to people like *Aunt Alma* and *Uncle Leo* in Fargo, North Dakota. We would like to refer to these new family members as in-laws rather than out-laws because we want the Lord to bless our relationship with them rather than having them as a source of conflict in our marriage. The Bible has some examples of in-law relationships. Let's take a look at what we can learn from them.

In the Book of Genesis we see that Rebekah wanted her son to choose the right spouse. This is not uncommon. Nearly every mother wants her son to marry a nice girl of which the family can be proud. Rebekah said to her husband Isaac, "I am weary of my life because of the daughters of Heth; if Jacob takes a wife of the daughters of Heth, like these who are the daughters of the land, what good will my life be to me" (Genesis 27:46)? Isaac and Rebekah must have also voiced their opinions about their hopes for a prospective mate for their firstborn son, Esau. The Word of God says:

> When Esau was forty years old, he took as wives Judith the daughter of Beeri the Hittite, and Basemath the daughter of Elon the Hittite. And they were a grief of mind to Isaac and Rebekah. (Genesis 26:34,35)

Now, we know that at this point in his life, Esau was old enough to make his own decisions. However, his choices were causing grief to his parents.

Jacob meets Rachel

Jacob heeded the advice of his parents and did not take "one of the daughters of Heth" for a wife. Instead, he left his family in Canaan, and traveled to Haran where the relatives of his mother lived. When he came near to Haran, he saw three flocks of sheep around a well, and he began to converse with the shepherds. The Bible says:

> Now while he was still speaking with them, Rachel came with her father's sheep, for she was a shepherdess. And it came to pass, when Jacob saw Rachel the daughter of Laban his mother's brother, and the sheep of Laban his mother's brother, that Jacob went near and rolled the stone from the well's mouth, and watered the flock of Laban his mother's brother. Then Jacob kissed Rachel, and lifted up his voice and wept. And Jacob told Rachel that he was her father's relative and that he was Rebekah's son. So she ran and told her father. (Genesis 29:9-12)

We see from this story that Jacob found the girl of his dreams, and he was not going to waste any time. Following the cultural practice of the day, he kissed her when they met, and they fell in love. Laban asked Jacob to stay and work for him because he was family. The Word of God says:

> Now Laban had two daughters: the name of the elder was Leah, and the name of the younger was Rachel. Leah's eyes were delicate, but Rachel was beautiful of form and appearance. Now Jacob loved Rachel; and he said, "I will serve you seven years for Rachel your younger daughter." And Laban said, "It is better that I give her to you than that I should give her to another man. Stay with me." So Jacob served seven years for Rachel, and they seemed but a few days to him because of the love he had for her. (Genesis 29:16-20)

Laban Exchanges Leah for Rachel

Jacob served his father-in-law for seven years feeding his flock and herds. This was to provide a dowry for the purchase of Rachel to be his wife. The Bible says:

> Then Jacob said to Laban, "Give me my wife, for my days are fulfilled, that I may go in to her." And Laban gathered together all the men of the place and made a feast. Now it came to pass in the evening, that he took Leah his daughter and brought her to Jacob; and he went in to her. So it came to pass in the morning, that behold, it was Leah. And he said to Laban, "What is this you have done to me? Was it not for Rachel that I served you? Why then have you deceived me?" And Laban said, "It must not be done so in our country, to give the younger before the firstborn." (Genesis 29:21-23,25,26)

Laban deceived Jacob in giving him Leah for a wife instead of Rachel. Jacob got back a little of what he deserved, however, because he deceived his twin brother Esau in the matter concerning his birthright before he ever left for Haran. (See Genesis 27:1-45. It is a great story.) Jacob was upset, but he worked seven more years for Rachel, and married her as well.

Keeping peace between families can be difficult, but the Scriptures say, "with God nothing will be impossible" (Luke 1:37). He can give us the love that can cross any barrier. Your in-laws-to-be may not be Christians, and they will not see things in the same light as you see them. They also may not understand some of the decisions you will make as a couple. This can become warring on any relationship, and must be a constant source of prayer.

There also can be areas of jealousy that arise between a parent and child. A mother may think, "This girl is spending too much time with my son. I hardly ever see him anymore," or "I am not ready for my daughter to get married. We are such good friends, and I do not want to lose her." And from this thought, your relationship with your in-laws can start out on a bad note.

Chocolate or Vanilla?

The stress in the relationship can intensify when we have to begin planning for the wedding. You and your fiancée may want a chocolate cake because it is your favorite, and your future mother-in-law wants you to choose vanilla because she is allergic to chocolate, and she thinks vanilla will satisfy more of the guests. In addition, you may not want alcohol at your reception, and your in-laws are demanding that you have it because they are worried about what their friends will think. There also can be struggles over how many guests each of your families can invite, or just the simple problem of personality conflicts between you. All of these can put stress on relationships.

How can we cope with all the people and opinions as we plan for The Big Day? We have to try to make the best of it, especially as Christians. Paul said:

> Be of the same mind toward one another. Do not set your mind on high things, but associate with the humble. Do not be wise in your own opinion. Repay no one evil for evil. Have regard for good things in the sight of all men. If it is possible, as much as depends on you, live peaceably with all men. (Romans 12:16-18)

We want to honor our parents, and listen to what they have to say, because they have wisdom that stems from experience. We need to tell them how much we appreciate them, and all that they have done for us. But, there also will come a time when we will need to leave and cleave, and kindly say, "We appreciate your opinion. We will take what you say into consideration, we would like to pray about it, and see what the Lord instructs us to do."

Moses and Jethro

God can give us wisdom through our in-laws, and that is why we always need to be open to criticism, or to change. In the Book of Exodus we read that Jethro heard that the Lord had brought His people out of Egypt, and he wanted to go and visit Moses and see how he was doing. He was excited to hear how God had delivered the Israelites from Pharaoh, and all of the miracles they had seen. The Bible says:

> And so it was, on the next day, that Moses sat to judge the people; and the people stood before Moses from morning until evening. So when Moses' father-in-law saw all that he did for the people, he said, "What is this thing that you are doing for the people? Why do you alone sit, and all the people stand before you from morning until evening?" And Moses said to his father-in-law, "Because the people come to me to inquire of God. When they have a difficulty, they come to me, and I judge between one and another; and I make known the statutes of God and His laws." So Moses' father-in-law said to him, "The thing that you do is not good. Both you and these people who are with you will surely wear yourselves out. For this thing is too much for you; you are not able to perform it by yourself." (Exodus 18:13-18)

Jethro counseled Moses to choose men who feared God to be rulers over the people. He told him that he should teach these men the statutes and laws that he himself had learned from God. He said:

> "And let them judge the people at all times. Then it will be that every great matter they shall bring to you, but every small matter they themselves shall judge. So it will be easier for you, for they will bear the burden with you." So Moses heeded the voice of his father-in-law and did all that he had said. (Exodus 18:22,24)

Jethro gave Moses great counsel that was obviously from the Lord. Jethro had a genuine concern for the well-being of Moses, and he wanted to lighten his burden. There may be times when we should heed the wisdom and insight of our parents. We need, however, to have a balance. Are they giving us godly counsel, or are their suggestions based on their own desires? Are they genuinely concerned about us, or do they want their own way? Remember the Bible says, "Trust in the LORD with all your heart, and lean not on your own understanding; in all your ways acknowledge Him, and He shall direct your paths" (Proverbs 3:5,6). We do not want to blindly obey our parents or in-laws, but we should consider what they have to say. Remember we are starting our own home, and our own traditions.

Moses was not full of pride, and he did not say, "Hey, I am married now. You need to mind your own business!" On the contrary, the Bible says, "Now the man Moses was very humble, more than all men who were on the face of the earth" (Numbers 12:3). He was teachable. God worked so many miracles through him, and yet he did not come across as a know-it-all. We need to follow his example with whomever we are speaking, especially if our in-laws are Christians.

The Story of Ruth

Another great example is found in the Book of Ruth. Ruth is a story of love, loyalty, and redemption. It is also a story of a bond between a mother-in-law and a daughter-in-law during a very tumultuous time in history. The story begins with a couple named Elimelech and Naomi, who moved with their two sons from Bethlehem to Moab because of a famine in the land. Shortly after they arrived, Elimelech died. The Bible says:

> Now [the sons] took wives of the women of Moab: the name of the one was Orpah, and the name of the other Ruth. And they dwelt there about ten years. Then both Mahlon and Chilion also died; so the woman survived her two sons and her husband. (Ruth 1:4,5)

After the famine was over in Bethlehem, Naomi decided to move back home. She told Orpah and Ruth to go back to their families in the land. After consideration, Orpah thought that was the best course of action. Ruth said, however:

> Entreat me not to leave you, or to turn back from following after you; for wherever you go, I will go; and wherever you lodge, I will lodge; your people shall be my people, and your God, my God. Where you die, I will die, and there will I be buried. The LORD do so to me, and more also, if anything but death parts you and me. (Ruth 1:16,17)

This is a very poetic vow, and many couples use these verses on their wedding invitation, but how many of us would be willing to do this for our in-laws? Let's say that your fiancée was from Germany, and you moved there after you got married. If they died, would you stay in Germany with your in-laws just because you loved them, and wanted to take care of them? Ruth was going to a place she had never been before, and she even said that nothing but death should part them. What a commitment!

I counseled a couple several months ago regarding this type of scenario. The man had an opportunity to go to school in the Midwest, and his fiancée said she would go with him after they got married. She knew it would be a challenge to leave a family she loved in California, but she had a joy to go. All of a sudden, her Christian parents intervened because they did not like the decision. They said to her fiancé, "Why are you taking our daughter away from us? This decision cannot be of God." The man needed to finish his schooling, and he had been accepted into a wonderful graduate program. These parents were trying to keep this couple from making their own decisions, and were only thinking of their loss. The girl was so torn that she and her fiancé almost called off the wedding! He wanted the will of God for his life, and was willing to postpone their wedding until he graduated. She finally submitted to what she felt God was telling her fiancé. They got married, and are doing great.

We need to remember that we are making a vow to our fiancée: "For better, or for worse; for richer, or for poorer; in sickness, and in health," and so forth. Maybe our commitment will take us away from family or friends, but God will sustain us if the decision is from Him! We lived overseas for only six months, and it was difficult for our families to adjust to writing letters and receiving infrequent phone calls. But we knew we made the choice God wanted us to make, and He took care of the rest.

God Will Reward Us

God does not take lightly the decisions we make for Him. He will reward us for any sacrifice that involves our obedience to His will. Jesus said:

> Assuredly, I say to you, there is no one who has left house or parents or brothers or wife or children, for the sake of the kingdom of God, who shall not receive many times more in this present time, and in the age to come everlasting life. (Luke 18:29,30)

He will bless us just as He blessed Ruth. At the conclusion of the book, she married a wealthy businessman named Boaz who became her kinsman redeemer because he was a relative of her husband. He said:

> It has been fully reported to me, all that you have done for your mother-in-law since the death of your husband, and how you have left your father and your mother and the land of your birth, and have come to a people whom you did not know before. The LORD repay your work, and a full reward be given you by the LORD God of Israel, under whose wings you have come for refuge. (Ruth 2:11,12)

God rewarded her for her faithfulness to her mother-in-law: She became the great grandmother of King David, and was in the lineage of Jesus Christ. Now that is a story where they lived happily ever after! God is good, and He will honor our godly choices as well.

There Will Be Challenges

We know that there will be sacrifices we will have to make as well as challenges ahead. The best thing we can remember is, "A friend loves at all times" (Proverbs 17:17). We need to think of our in-laws as friends, even if they are not Christians. God can use us to be a witness to them. The Bible also says, A man who wants friends, "must himself be friendly" (Proverbs 18:24). If we want our in-laws to be kind to us, we need to be kind to them. If we want them to be flexible with us regarding our wedding plans, are we flexible as well? It works both ways. If we want a good relationship with our in-laws, we have to cultivate one. I recently received a call from a woman who was distraught about her future daughter-in-law. The girl was unkind to her future in-laws, and was very controlling. She did not want them to be a part of their lives, and she was doing everything within her power to keep her fiancé from his parents. While we recognize that we will have many challenges in our relationships, it does not negate our Christian responsibility to love. Here are some questions we can ask ourselves:

- Do we respect our future or current in-laws?

- Do we treat them kindly, or do we have an attitude?

- Do we try to do all we can to make for peace in our relationship with them?

- Do we pray for them?

We can glean a lot from the lives of Moses and Ruth: they were humble, and did not demand their own way; they received instruction, and they were open to change; they responded to their in-laws in love, and sacrificed their own desires. We also need to be open to the Lord in using our in-laws in various areas of our lives. We have heard people say, "It is such a blessing that my in-laws do not live nearby." It is unfortunate that they feel this way because there can be many blessings that arise from a good relationship with the family of our spouse. Look what Ruth would have forfeited if she had such an attitude. Let's not be quick to burn our bridges if we have had some setbacks. We need to pray about it, and try to make amends. We will only have a richer relationship with our in-laws and peace in our home if we do.

Review Questions

In-Laws

1. What does the word "in-law" mean to you?

   _____

   _____

   _____

   _____

   _____

2. After reviewing the stories of Moses and Ruth, what are some of the key ingredients we need in our relationships with our in-laws? (See Ephesians 4:32 to help you with your answer.)

   _____

   _____

   _____

   _____

   _____

3. Describe the ideal in-law from your perspective.

   _____

   _____

   _____

   _____

   _____

4. What has been the response of your parents concerning your plans to get married?

_____

_____

_____

_____

_____

5. What opinion do you think your future or current in-laws have of you?

_____

_____

_____

_____

_____

6. How much time do you plan on spending with your parents or your in-laws?

_____

_____

_____

_____

_____

7. Describe the plans you have for your first Thanksgiving and Christmas, as a married couple?

_____

_____

_____

_____

_____

8. List some attributes you appreciate about the parents of your fiancée or spouse.

   a) _____

   b) _____

   c) _____

   d) _____

9. Becoming a part of the family of your fiancée can be wonderful, and at the same time it can be overwhelming. List your concerns, and share them with one another.

   _____

   _____

   _____

   _____

   _____

10. What are some ways you can express the love of Christ to your parents and future in-laws?

    a) _____

    b) _____

    c) _____

Notes

_____

_____

_____

_____

_____

_____

_____

_____

_____

_____

_____

_____

_____

_____

_____

_____

_____

_____

_____

_____

_____

_____

Notes

CHAPTER NINE

Remarriage

Deal with the Past

In this day and age we realize that some of the people reading this will be those who have already been married previously. Some have gone through a painful divorce, while others have suffered the loss of a spouse. In each case, both are facing the prospect of remarriage. If God has opened the door for us to get remarried, we are taking a major step. There are essentials that need to be discussed before we make this new commitment.

Before we move forward, we need to look from where we have come, and the circumstances that affected our union. What has brought us to this point in our lives? We do not want to bring the past into our new relationship; however, we do need to be honest with one another about what happened, and who we are today. Perhaps there are some issues we have never confronted. We pray that through this chapter, the answers will become clear. We will discuss them, and allow the Lord to turn our stumbling blocks into steppingstones.

We know from the Word of God that we are not to let the past hinder our future, because the Lord has forgiven us if we have asked Him. The Apostle Paul said:

> Brethren, I do not count myself to have apprehended; but one thing I do, forgetting those things which are behind and reaching forward to those things which are ahead, I press toward the goal for the prize of the upward call of God in Christ Jesus. (Philippians 3:13,14)

We need to allow the Lord to deal with us regarding our past because we do not want to bring any baggage with us into our new life. We serve a God who can and will restore us. (See Joel 2:25.)

If you have been divorced, and have not dealt with all of the ramifications of what happened in your past, you need to ask yourself these questions:

- Why did you leave your former spouse?

- Were you a Christian at the time?

- Did you have Biblical grounds to get divorced?

- What role did you play in the break-up?

- Have you given God enough time to heal your heart?

If you have been widowed, you need to ask yourself these questions:

- What kind of relationship did you have?

- Have you taken enough time to grieve over the loss of your spouse?

- Do you find yourself comparing your current relationship with the past?

Be Honest With One Another

In order to help us in our new relationship, we need to try to understand what our fiancée went through before they met us. What were the difficulties? We may have faced various issues with our former spouse including terminal illness, tragedy, anger, lying, alcohol, abuse, adultery, or abandonment. We need to be honest with ourselves and with one another regarding our past, as we discussed in Chapter One. One man we talked to was devastated because his wife left him for someone else which terminated the marriage. A few years later, he started dating a woman, and they began to have problems. He realized that he had never dealt with his insecurities from the former relationship. He was still living with mistrust and fear, and his girlfriend was becoming concerned. He always wanted to know where she was during the day, and they were not even engaged at this point. We prayed together several times, and God showed them that they needed to deal with these areas before they went any deeper in their relationship. Recognizing our weaknesses is the first step. Once we have realized where the problems lie, we can pray about them, and we can ask others to intercede for us in prayer. James said, "The effective, fervent prayer of a righteous man avails much" (James 5:16). This couple waited until they both felt peaceful about what God was doing in their lives, they dealt with their problems, and they are happily married today.

Ask God For Wisdom

As we interact together, and issues arise that we do not understand, we need to ask the Lord for wisdom. James says, "If any of you lacks wisdom, let him ask of God, who gives to all liberally and without reproach, and it will be given to him" (James 1:5). If we are in an argument, or one of us has an attitude, we need to go to the Lord about it. There can be issues from our past that cause us to respond that way. Ask the Lord why there is anger, fear, or criticism. He wants to give us insight regarding ourselves as well as with one another. This wonderful promise is ours if we will just ask Him:

> Call to Me, and I will answer you, and show you great and
> mighty things, which you do not know. (Jeremiah 33:3)

Once the Lord reveals the answers to us, we can deal with them. We can go through each issue systematically and thoroughly discuss it. As we interact we need to remember the instruction from Chapter Five: We are to attack the problem, and not one another.

There are going to be people from our past with whom we will have to deal on a regular basis, and seeing these people can evoke feelings and emotions within us. We need to be on guard and in prayer for each other so that we do not enter into fleshly or verbal warfare. (See Ephesians 6:12.) One person with whom we might have to interact is our ex-spouse, especially if we have had children together. This can be a challenge. We know a couple who got married several years ago. The husband was married before, and has a child from his former marriage. His current wife deals with his former wife on a biweekly basis because she arranges the time when the child stays with them. There are difficulties, but they are getting through it with the help of the Lord. She hoped when they first got married, that she would not have to see the ex-wife, or talk to her. Now she realizes that this woman is a part of her life, and she needs to get used to it.

We need to keep our former spouse in the proper perspective. If they are still trying to control us, or manipulate us in some way, that needs to come to an end. We need to limit the communication to discussing our children, or the financial necessities. Do what is needed to maintain amicability, and that is all. We prayed with a man who had been divorced, and had recently remarried. His former wife still had the key to his home, and would come and go as she pleased. She would often sit down at the table, and begin visiting with them, and she would even invite herself to dinner on occasion. She was causing a lot of conflict because the husband would not communicate any wrongdoing to her. He was not protecting his new relationship! He did not want to confront her, and his new wife became bitter because of it. That is not what God intended. Our husband-to-be or our wife-to-be is our priority now; they are our ministry before the Lord.

Think About the Children

Children are an important factor in remarriage, and we do not want to neglect them while we are seeking fulfillment in a new relationship. Blended families can be a challenge for us. A child may say, "I do not have to do what you want me to because you are not my dad," or, "This was *our* home before you moved in." This can cause stress in our lives. We need to fully discuss each situation with one another as it arises, and the ramifications each choice we make has on our children. I recently read of a divorce case where a judge ruled that a child was to live with the mother for one year and with the father the next. I thought, "How sad!" The paper said the ruling was in the best interests of the child. As parents, we need to be praying for our children on a regular basis. After all, they are not just children; they are little *people* with thoughts, emotions, and fears. They need to know that their feelings are being considered as we make plans for the future.

What is our role as a parent? We discussed the roles of husbands and wives in Chapter Two, and our first ministry we know is to our new wife, or our new husband. But we also have our ministry to our children. Before we take our vows before the Lord, our family, and our friends, we need to talk about how we are going to incorporate our children into our new lives, and we need to come to an agreement regarding some basics:

• How will we raise them?

• What methods will we use in order to discipline them?

• Do we agree on visitations, vacations, and holidays?

• Do we feel comfortable regarding the financial agreement we have made concerning them?

We Need to Be Servants

We discussed the importance of being a servant in Chapter Two, and this is where we begin in marriage, and in parenting. Paul said, "Let each of you look out not only for his own interests, but also for the interests of others" (Philippians 2:4). If we have this type of attitude with our children and our step-children, we are going to make an impact on their lives. They need to know that we care about them, and that we want to build a relationship with them. Maybe they never received the love they desired from the parent who left the marriage, or perhaps they are still struggling from the death of their parent. We can change the direction of their lives, and be used by the Lord to bring them healing and wholeness.

I officiated over the marriage of a blended family not too long ago, and what a witness they were to me. The man had three little children, and the woman had a six-year-old. They all interacted so beautifully together as I met with them several times over the course of a year. It was special to see them ministering to one another. It was obvious that this couple loved the Lord, and each other. The woman treated all of the children the same—as if they were hers. The couple devoted a lot of energy to having quality family time, and the children loved it. The wedding was in January, and the wife died in May of the same year. She was only thirty-five years old, and I was asked to do her funeral. It was so obvious that this woman had made a marked impact on these children even though she had only known them for about two years. They all wanted to participate in the funeral service. They shared what a great mother she was to them, and how much they loved her. They said that they really enjoyed the meals she cooked, and the way she read Bible stories to them every night before they went to bed. This woman was an example of a servant because she put all of her children before herself. There was no favoritism between her love for her natural child, and that of the step-children. She had been a powerful witness of the love of Jesus Christ, even in the short time she was alive to minister to them.

I think it is important for us to consider the witness of this woman, and our attitude toward our children as we consider marrying again. We do not often realize that children so often bear the effects of divorce or death. We decided not to stay in our former relationship for one reason or another, and now we have found a new love. We are blessed while our children are being pulled back and forth trying to cope with the decisions made around them. Sometimes they are just too young to even process all of the information, and they react with indifference. Our role is to ferret out what is going on inside their minds, whether they are two or twenty years old. As we invest in their lives, the Lord will use us to change the course of how they feel about God, themselves, and marriage.

Review Questions

Remarriage

In order for God to "do a new thing" for us, we must be willing to let go of the former things. (See Isaiah 43:18,19,25.) Everyone who has been properly divorced may remarry according to the Word of God.

1. If you have been divorced, was it for Biblical grounds? How have you reconciled with God in regard to this?

   _____

   _____

   _____

   _____

   _____

2. Have you done everything possible to reconcile with your former spouse before taking this step to remarry? (See Romans 12:18 and 2 Corinthians 5:18.)

   _____

   _____

   _____

   _____

   _____

3. List the things for which you have had to forgive (or need to forgive) your former spouse.

   a) _____

   b) _____

c) _____

d) _____

e) _____

4. Make a list of the things you have had to forgive (or need to forgive) in the individuals who had a part in the dissolution of your marriage. (See Ephesians 4:32.)

a) _____

b) _____

c) _____

5. What sins have you confessed to God and others, in regard to your part in your marital breakup? How did you make it right with God, as well as with the others? What sins still need to be confessed? (See Matthew 7:1-5.)

_____

_____

_____

_____

_____

6. How do you know that you have waited on the Lord for His timing to remarry? (See Isaiah 40:31.)

_____

_____

_____

_____

_____

7. God has a standard for remarriage which is found in 2 Corinthians 6:14. In light of this Scripture, describe how you know that you are spiritually compatible with your fiancée.

_____

_____

_____

_____

_____

8. The ideal, in the eyes of God, is *one life, one marriage*. He extends His mercy to us by permitting divorce and remarriage. There will be consequences, and many issues involving you and your children must be prayerfully considered. What is the view of God in relation to:

a) how you deal with your ex-spouse? (See Luke 10:27.)

_____

_____

_____

_____

b) the grandparents and extended family?

_____

_____

_____

_____

c) visitations, vacations, and holidays? (See Romans 12:18.)

_____

_____

_____

_____

9. Are you both in agreement concerning the financial obligations incurred regarding the children and alimony? How does it line up with the standard God has set? (See 1 Timothy 5:8.)

_____

_____

_____

_____

_____

10. What is your plan for raising your children? How does it comply with the teaching you find in the Word of God? (See Deuteronomy 6:5-9.)

_____

_____

_____

_____

11. Have you discussed your new roles? Make a list of them, and implement a plan with which you both agree. An example would be: What do you want your step-children to call you? (See Ephesians 6:1-4.)

_____

_____

_____

_____

12. The Bible says that God does not show partiality to anyone. (See James 2:1-4.) What are ways that you can include your children and step-children into your new life?

_____

_____

13. Each remarriage has unique challenges. List some potential conflicts, and find a Scripture that applies to each conflict on your list.

1) _____

_____

2) _____

_____

3) _____

_____

4) _____

_____

5) _____

_____

14. Knowing that no one is able to fill the shoes of your deceased spouse, do you find yourself comparing your fiancée with them? If so, how?

_____

_____

_____

_____

_____

15. Make a list of the qualities you admire in your fiancée or spouse, and focus on these attributes. (See Philippians 4:8.)

_____

_____

_____

_____

_____

Notes

Notes

_____
_____
_____
_____
_____
_____
_____
_____
_____
_____
_____
_____
_____
_____
_____
_____
_____
_____
_____
_____
_____
_____
_____

Conclusion

God ordained marriage from the beginning. He saw that it was not good for man to be alone, so He brought a lovely woman to complete him. God is the one who instituted marriage, and He has plans for our lives and our futures as we serve Him together. The key ingredient in every marriage needs to be *the Lord* as Solomon said, "A threefold cord is not quickly broken" (Ecclesiastes 4:12). God is the one who is going to keep our marriage alive, and help us to be the husband and wife that He wants us to be.

Throughout the Word of God we find instruction for living. Jesus said, "I have come that [you] may have life, and that [you] may have it more abundantly" (John 10:10). In order to enjoy life, we need to be obedient to the Word of God. We have covered some of the potential obstacles that can arise in marriage. However, these should not deter us from the joy that awaits us. Marriage is a tremendous blessing! The instruction we presented in this book can be likened to information we would receive if we were to embark on a river rafting adventure. We need to understand that there are rules to follow before we begin. The first requirement is that we listen to our tour guide. He will give us explicit directions for working together with our team members, and what we are to do in case of an emergency. We must wear a life jacket, and so forth. It is important that we listen, and follow through with action. Now, we do not hear this and say, "Forget it! I am not going river rafting if there are rules to follow." No, that would be ridiculous! We know that the rules are instituted for our safety, and will only enhance the fun as we journey down the white water.

So it is with marriage. God has given us an instruction manual in His Word to help us through this journey of marriage. He has spoken, and it is important that we listen. His instruction is for our good, and it will enhance our union. Marriage is so exciting. It is just like river rafting. We never know what is up ahead. It is full of surprises! There will be ups and downs, but with God as our Captain, we can enjoy the adventure as He guides us.

We have experienced such joy and fun throughout our marriage. This is not to say that we have not had our vicissitudes, but God has been there to help us through the difficulties as we have continued to seek Him. It has been so much fun, and we are more in love today than when we first met. We only wish that we could be married throughout eternity. We know that there is no marriage in heaven so we will have to be content with being best friends on earth, and spending eternity together.

Our prayer is that you will come to experience the joy and fulfillment that God intended for you in this adventure called marriage!

Recommended Reading

Adams, Jay E. Christian Living in the Home. Phillipsburg: Presbyterian and Reformed Publishing Co., 1972.

Brodersen, Brian Spiritual Warfare. Costa Mesa: The Word for Today, 1995.

Burkett, Larry with Michael E. Taylor Money in Marriage: A Biblical Approach. Chicago: Moody Press Edition, 1999.

Burkett, Larry The Family Budget Workbook: Gaining Control of Your Personal Finances. Chicago: Northfield Publishing, 1993.

Carr, Steve Married And How To Stay That Way! Phoenix: ACW Press, 1998.

Miller, Basil George Muller: A Man of Faith and Miracles. Minneapolis: Bethany Fellowship, Inc., 1941.

Smith, Chuck Effective Prayer Life. Costa Mesa: The Word for Today, 2000.

Stonebraker, Bill Spiritual Warfare in Marriage: Winning the Battle for a Good Marriage. Honolulu: Calvary Chapel, 2000.

Talley, Jim A. and Bobbie Reed Too Close Too Soon. Nashville: Thomas Nelson Publishers, 1990.

Bibliography

1 Abigail Van Buren, "Dear Abby," <u>The Orange County Register</u> 27 March 2000: B2.

2 Gallup Research Corporation, <u>Commissioned Research on Evangelical Christians,</u> May 1991.

3 Warren Wiersbe, <u>Be Dynamic</u>: Experience the same power that motivated early Christians (Wheaton: SP Publications, 1987) 84.

4 Ibid.

5 Steve Carr, <u>Married and How to Stay That Way!</u> (Phoenix: ACW Press, 1998) 140,141.

6 Willard F. Harley, <u>His Needs/Her Needs</u>, (Grand Rapids: Fleming H. Revell, 1986) 12,13.

7 "All the Way My Savior Leads Me." By Fanny J. Crosby and Robert Lowry. Public Domain.

To obtain additional copies of this workbook, or the *Two Shall Become One* audio tape series contact:

The Word for Today
P.O. Box 8000
Costa Mesa, CA 92628

or call 1-800-272-9673